DIAMONDS ARE FOREVER

ARTISTS AND
WRITERS
ON BASEBALL

**Edited by Peter H. Gordon,
with Sydney Waller and Paul Weinman**

INTRODUCTION BY DONALD HALL

From the exhibition
organized by the New York State Museum
in association with the
Smithsonian Institution Traveling Exhibition Service.
The exhibition and its tour
are made possible by·a grant from
American Express Company.

Chronicle Books • San Francisco

Published by Chronicle Books
in association with:
Smithsonian Institution Traveling Exhibition Service and
New York State Museum, Albany

Design by Dare Porter/Graphic Design, San Francisco

Printed in Japan by Dai Nippon Printing Co., Ltd., Tokyo.

Diamonds Are Forever: Artists and Writers on Baseball has been
organized by the New York State Museum in association with
the Smithsonian Institution Traveling Exhibition Service.
The exhibition and its tour are made possible by a grant from
American Express Company.

Library of Congress Cataloging in Publication Data
Diamonds are forever.
   Published in association with Smithsonian Institution
Traveling Exhibition Service   and New York State
Museum, Albany.
   1. Baseball—Literary collections.   2. American
literature—20th century.   3. Baseball in art.
4. Baseball in art—Exhibitions.   I. Gordon, Peter H.
PS509.B37D5   1987   810'.9'355   87-14585
ISBN 0-87701-475-2
ISBN 0-87701-468-X (pbk.)

Distributed in Canada by
Raincoast Books
112 East 3rd Avenue
Vancouver, B.C.
V5T 1C8

10 9 8 7 6 5 4 3 2 1

Chronicle Books
San Francisco, California

Contents

Preface

A reviewer once distilled the essence of a book about baseball in these terms: "It's about youth and dreams and fame and success and failure and inspiration and devotion." Those few words go a long way toward explaining why baseball matters so much to so many.

Whether the game appeals to us because we once played softball after school and dreamed of being the next Babe Ruth, or simply because we savor the taste of a hot dog and an ice-cold drink at the ballpark as we cheer for the home team—the magic and myth of baseball is ingrained in our society, and always will be.

That is why we felt it was particularly appropriate for American Express to sponsor this uniquely American exhibition, and we extend our thanks to the New York State Museum and the Smithsonian Institution Traveling Exhibition Service for giving us the opportunity to do so.

Diamonds Are Forever lets us see baseball from an artist's perspective so that we can explore the cultural, as well as the popular phenomenon of the sport. The artists and writers represented here are among the best of America. Through their paintings, drawings, sculpture and writings, they show us the pride, determination, joy and pathos of the game, its players and its fans.

James D. Robinson III
Chairman and Chief Executive Officer
American Express Company

Foreword

Baseball is not just a game, but a coordinated strategy. It is a combination of skill, talent, luck, mutual encouragement, and hard work. Each year a Most Valuable Player (MVP) in each league is recognized for outstanding contributions to the team, but the truth is that no single player can win a game or series alone. Winning requires a balance of strong offense and good defense, fine pitching and timely hitting. These elements work together to create a winning season.

Baseball is a team effort, and so are exhibitions.

Diamonds Are Forever has the right balance. The New York State Museum contributed the curatorial expertise which blended well with the experience and batting record of the Smithsonian Institution Traveling Exhibition Service (SITES). The host museums on the national tour and this book published by Chronicle Books extend this collaborative project to what we hope will be expanded audiences. It is all being made possible by generous support from American Express Company.

Like avid baseball fans, we cheer this talented combination for bringing home a winner!

Martin E. Sullivan
Director
New York State Museum

Peggy A. Loar
Director
Smithsonian Institution
Traveling Exhibition Service

Introduction: The View from the Bench

What is it about baseball?

The question seemed so simple at first. Was it the history . . . the great moments, the teams, the players? We tossed exhibit ideas back and forth. One idea was a look at baseball in New York City during the 1950s—those glorious heyday years of the Yankees, Dodgers, and Giants. "Wait 'Til Next Year" was the title. Nothing came of it. The purely historical nature of the project didn't interest me, and Bob Sullivan (my manager) was too busy. Besides, I'm a Red Sox fan. Think of my agony researching the Yankees.

Then in 1985, a friend gave me a copy of *Fathers Playing Catch With Sons: Essays on Sport (Mostly Baseball)* by Donald Hall. It's a wonderful set of essays, and in the one entitled "Proseball: Sports, Stories, and Style," Hall discusses literature about baseball and includes a section from John Updike's famous essay, "Hub Fans Bid Kid Adieu" (included in its entirety in this book). Updike's piece deals with Ted Williams, his last game at Fenway, and especially his last time at bat—in which he hit a home run. Updike writes:

It was in the books while it was still in the sky. Brandt ran back to the deepest corner of the outfield grass, the ball descended beyond his reach and struck in the crotch where the bullpen met the wall, bounced chunkily, and vanished.

Like a feather caught in a vortex, Williams ran around the square of bases at the center of our beseeching screaming. He ran as he always ran out home runs— hurriedly, unsmiling, head down, as if our praise were a storm of rain to get out of. He didn't tip his cap. Though we thumped, wept, and chanted "We want Ted" for minutes after he hid in the dugout, he did not come back. Our noise for some seconds passed beyond excitement into a kind of immense open anguish, a wailing, a cry to be saved. But immortality is nontransferable. The papers said that the other players, and even the umpires on the field, begged him to come out and acknowledge us in some way, but he refused. Gods do not answer letters.

Whew! After reading that passage, I too remembered that day . . . I grew up in Rhode Island and, of course, was a Red Sox fan. By September 28th of that year, 1960, my school's baseball season was over. We were into the football and, for me, soccer season. Knowing it was Williams's last home game, we had all brought transistor radios to JV practice. So I heard that famous home run, and

later, saw it over and over on the TV news. That event was a part of *my* experience, just as it was a part of Updike's experience. But Updike's insight into that moment transformed it, and made my experience and memory of it something wholly new.

But isn't that the "job" of the artist? They take those experiences that many of us have and transform them into something new—into paintings and poems and essays that challenge us, or delight us, or touch us so deeply that we're convinced there's magic going on there somewhere. That "transformation" by the artist is not just technique. The artist has that rare ability to make the ordinary, extraordinary; that rare ability to help us see and experience with "new eyes." So that the next time we step out from the walkway to our seats at Yankee Stadium, it looks to us "just like that Fasanella painting" and like Lesley Hazleton, we "gasp at the perfect greenness of it." Their art becomes a part of us, a part of our experience.

I knew then that our baseball exhibition must be about the artist's and writer's personal insight into baseball, not the art or social historian's analytical view of the game.

Eight years ago, I organized an exhibition entitled "The New York Landscape" that combined the work of poets and artists. In that exhibition, we selected poems, then invited artists to respond to the poems. This time, we chose both the visual and the literary selections, making the juxtapositions ourselves. It was our goal not to have one illustrate the other. We tried for an equal integrity to both words and images, creating a dialogue where they would respond to, amplify, and illuminate each other without intruding on the viewer's experience.

Next, we needed to focus the exhibition on a single, central question . . . the question we wanted to answer *through* the exhibition. There was so much material, so many different directions we could take the material. We wrote down all the possible questions on index cards: one question per card. The list was long, but we kept returning to one very basic question: "What is it about baseball that fascinates and touches us so deeply?" Why does baseball hold, as Wilfrid Sheed has written, "a reserved seat in the American psyche"?

We know some of the answers ourselves because of our own experiences as parents of little-leaguers, as armchair umpires, or as weekend softball players (many of us over the hill). Yet, while many of our experiences, feelings, and memories about baseball are shared in common, the creative ability to express them is not.

And so in our exhibition, we turned to artists and writers (some hall-of-famers, some all-stars, many first-string veterans, and even a few rookies) to help us answer our question.

Finally we needed to structure this mass of material sensibly. What is it about baseball? Well, for these artists and writers, it seemed to be something about . . .

The Place: Yankee Stadium; Chaney Field—Home of the Waldorf Little League; infields of hard, baked dirt full of pebbles; and ball parks like Fenway —changeless and symmetrical.

The Equipment: A Louisville Slugger; a baseball, that perfect object for a man's hand; the smell of varnish and leather; and a well-worn and well-used, older brother's glove.

The Players: The heroes and the has-beens; the great memorable teams and those frustrating perennial losers; and the daydream of making that impossible catch.

The Action: The pitcher winding like a clock—the batter tense and waiting; the ball and baserunner both heading towards home; and the crowd, rising as one when the ball's hit deep.

"Something Else": Fathers and sons; the sounds and smells of a summer night; listening to the game on the car radio; and the cosmic struggles

that all games can come to represent.

Basically then, that was the way this idea and project developed. Fortunately, we had a good team on the field to bring it home. If I had the ball on the pitcher's mound, Bob Sullivan was back behind the plate, calling the game, positioning the players, and generally taking charge. And as any fan knows, you can't win without being strong up the middle. We had Sydney Waller at second. Good glove, moves well to the left. She did major league work on the visual component of the show. At shortstop, defying laws of gravity (and sometimes society), was Paul Weinman—a superb poet and the Phil Rizzuto of baseball's literature. In fact, we had help from so many people, there's a separate page at the end of the book to say thanks to our deep bench.

What is it about baseball that touches us so deeply? Turn these pages. Read Updike, Hall, Keillor, and Kennedy. Look at Dow, Lawrence, and Rauschenberg. (Wait! Maybe get some peanuts or a hotdog first!) These artists and writers give us a whole range of answers to our question. They also give us the chance to share, to remember, to dream . . . and to discover new answers of our own.

Peter H. Gordon,
New York State Museum

Shapes of the Game Forever   by Donald Hall

For some of us the game is Fenway Park, with Roger Clemens and Oil Can Boyd; with Billy Bucks, Jim Rice, and perennial failure; with Fenway's classy old-fashioned city-scape shape, set in the middle of turnpikes and factories, tenements, schools, and shops. Or the game's shape may be Dodger Stadium, sculpted out of a stolen ravine under the phlegmy dome of Los Angeles. It is even the dread duplicate shapes, Andy Warhol replicas, of Pittsburgh and Cincinnati. At baseball's heart is a repeated shape; the flatted diamond stays the same forever.

As we fly over Southern California we see below the ten thousand patterns of basepaths-and-grass. High over Maine forests, over deserts of Arizona, even over Rocky wastes, we spy from our easy chair, elevated to the height of five miles, the small landscape and geometry of baseball. Even over Italy and Japan, even over China, we see beneath us the footprints of the game. World enough we have, from five miles up, as the airplane contributes eternity's viewpoint to the human imagination. From our vertical perch at least we confirm the horizontal game.

As when we see, rising from the flat greenfield of the game, hovering above the bleachers, the great highrise of the team's

city. The city brings grass and horizontality into itself by means of the game, reassuringly touches itself with the earth's honest flatness staked out against the earth's curve.

World enough we have, but time is another matter, as Einstein liked to say. Our time is all acceleration, progressive and geometrical. If our grandfather's diamond is ours, his glove is not nor is his bat. His glove looks like Mickey Mouse's only skinnier; his bat shows the mark where he turned it on a lathe. It's true that the swing remains—as we can tell from old images: The line of that swing connects us by its sibilant swoop, an S of beauty, as leg sweeps up through trunk to arms extended into bat that exists to extend arm. This line by necessity runs counter to the pitcher's line whose front leg rears and plunges, whose rear leg soars, whose arm rips mightily forward following-through to *put something* on the whitest ball, or "spheroid" as the poet says. These lines of force and this forceful rhetoric wind us back, back to our grandfather's game, back to *his* grandfather's game who played before Shiloh.

We remember, we memorialize, we invent: *forever*, as we like to think. The daily life—so fragile and frail—we make as permanent as geometry and

bronze; we make a bronze geometry of heroes. When Pausanias, a medical man of the Athenian persuasion who flourished in the second century after Christ, travelled over Greece and wrote about it, he looked far back to heroic times of his city's greatness (Pericles, Thucydides, Plato, Sophocles) seven hundred years before his own. He spoke proudly of the Greek traces and ruins, as today a European might write about thirteenth-century cathedrals. Pausanias named ten thousand sculptures that no longer exist, gods and heroes; he commemorated the names of thousands of carved perpetual great athletes and copied down ancient poetic inscriptions recounting their triumphs. As Pindar, 500 B.C., wrote odes about wrestlers and runners, so the classic sculptors carved and modeled likenesses of a sixteen-year-old girl who won her race and of a man who won two thousand races and kept running at fifty.

It is by baseball, and not by other American sports, that our memories bronze themselves. Other sports change too fast, rise with the highrise, mutate for mutability, modify to modernize. By baseball we join hands with the long line of forefathers and with the dead. Thus a player now in his prime looks back fifteen years to when he played semi-pro at thirteen in Mississippi. ("The umpires would have whiskey bottles sticking out of their pockets.") He looks back because baseball occupies historical time, and because Dennis Boyd's father, who ran the Meridian A's, told his son that his grandfather also played here "around the turn of the century," when he wasn't allowed in the white man's leagues. Here Willie Boyd himself pitched to Hank Aaron and Willy Mays. Here six Boyd brothers of Dennis's generation played together on one team.

Maybe I've seen this familiar diamond from five miles up, dear flat patch of green and brown. Maybe I see it now, maybe you do too, for it is now and then, the prevailing baseball field. The shape endures and the Can plays the forever game, as he rambles with the shape of it: "I play the game for the love of it, just like my father and my friends, their fathers and their friends.

"I want to last a long time and pitch grayhaired, like Gaylord Perry and Satchel.

"I'd like to pitch forever, I guess."

Andrew Radcliffe
The Baseball Game, 1986
Oil on canvas

Joel Meyerowitz
Busch Stadium and the
Arch, 1978
Photograph

Yankee Stadium;
Chaney Field–Home of the
Waldorf Little League; infields of
hard, baked dirt full of pebbles;
and ball parks like Fenway–
changeless and symmetrical.

Ralph Fasanella

Night Game–Yankee
Stadium (Detail), 1961
Oil on canvas

Cristos Gianakos
Six Altered Baseball Stadium
  Post Cards (Detail), 1985
Collage

Andy Jurinko
Wrigley Field, 1983
Charcoal and pastel on paper

Doubtless, there are better places to spend summer days, summer nights, than in ball parks. Doubtless.

Nevertheless, decades after a person has stopped collecting bubble-gum cards, he can still discover himself collecting ball parks. And not just the stadiums, but their surrounding neighborhoods, their smells, their special seasons and moods.

Thomas Boswell, *from*
How Life Imitates the
World Series

John Kennard
New York, NY, 1983
Photograph

Jane Irish
Shea Stadium is the New York Mets
and the New York Mets are
Shea Stadium, 1984
Egg tempera on board/cardboard

Lewis Hine
Playground in a Tenement Alley, Boston, 1909
Photograph

It was a sunny, dry September Sunday—the kind of day that can convince an unsuspecting stranger that New York is a wonderful place to spend the summer. I was fresh off the plane from Israel. It was only my second day in the United States, but my friends here had made the shocked discovery that I

had never even seen a baseball diamond. So they took me out to the ball game. Thurman Munson had been killed in a plane crash a few weeks before, and the Yankees weren't going to be in any World Series that year. But this particular Sunday had been declared Catfish Hunter day. Ole Catfish was retiring, and New York had turned out for him.

Maybe it was in comparison with the parched browns of Israel at summer's end. Maybe it was the combined smell of hot dogs and marijuana drifting over the stands. Maybe it was the light. All I know for sure is that when I emerged from the tunnel and stood there in the first tier, looking out over home base, I gasped at the perfect greenness of it. So this was a diamond.

What happened then was everything I expected from America. A brass band, heavy on the epaulets and the drums. High-stepping marching girls in white rubber bootees and pompons, throwing silver plywood rifles twisting into the air. A whole ceremony right on the field, including Catfish's mother, wife and two young boys, and of course Catfish himself—the archetype of the huntin'-shootin'-fishin' man. Speeches were made and messages read out from presidents of various

organizations, including one President called Jimmy Carter. Gifts were hauled, driven and led out onto the field (television sets, Toyota cars and a live elephant, respectively). And then came a hush as Catfish approached the microphone.

"There's three men shoulda been here today," he said. "One's my pa"—riotous applause—"one's the scout that signed me"—more riotous applause—"and the third one"—pause—"is Thurman Munson." Riot. Fifty thousand people up on their feet and roaring, including my friends. The fifty thousand and first—myself—looked on in bewilderment. I missed Catfish's next sentence, but I'll never forget the last one of that brief speech. "Thank you, God," he said, "for giving me strength, and making me a ballplayer."

And suddenly I too was up on my feet and cheering. It was the perfect American day, the perfect American place, the perfect American sentence. That combination of faith and morality, sincerity and naiveté, was everything my Old-World preconceptions had led me to expect, and as I watched Catfish walk off the field into the sunset of the Baseball Hall of Fame, leading his little boy with one hand and the elephant with the other, I felt that I had had my first glimpse of a mythical place called America.

Three hot dogs, two bags of peanuts, three glasses of beer and nine innings later, I was amazed to find out how much I already knew about baseball. In fact I'd played a simpler form of it as a schoolgirl in England, where it was called rounders and was played exclusively by rather upperclass young ladies in the best public schools, which in England of course means the best private schools. Yet though we played on asphalt and used hard cricket balls, and played with all the savagery that enforced good breeding can create, we never dreamed of such refinements as I saw that afternoon. The exhilaration of sliding into base! That giant paw of the glove! The whole principle of hustle! A world awaits the well-bred young Englishwoman in the ballpark. But for me the most splendid of these splendors was to watch the American language being acted out.

Though I knew no Americans when I lived in England—those were the years when America was still considered a brash black sheep of the family, so to speak, and was not mentioned in polite society—I

Ralph Fasanella

Night Game—Yankee Stadium, 1961

Oil on canvas

came to know many in the years I lived in Israel. And since they were the only people with whom I spoke English, I picked up their language. I could touch base, give a ballpark figure, strike out and reach first base long before I ever realized that these were baseball terms. I could be out of the ball game, let alone out of the ballpark. I could play ball—even hardball when I had to. There were times when I climbed the walls, and accused others of being off the wall. And it seemed I had a talent for throwing the occasional curve ball in an argument. . . .

That September Sunday in Yankee Stadium, the American language loaded the bases and gave me a grand slam home run. It came alive for me, and with

it, American culture. Baseball was suddenly my code to understanding this culture, the key to the continent. And I knew that I'd really arrived in America one rainy afternoon a couple of years later, the kind of afternoon that lends itself to sitting at your desk, staring out the window and daydreaming. Slowly, I realized that I had just emerged smiling from the classic 10-year-old-boy's all-American fantasy: seventh game of the World Series, three runs down, bases loaded, two out, and I'm up at bat. I take a strike on the first pitch. The crowd is roaring. Another strike on the second pitch. The crowd roars even louder. And then comes the third pitch, right where I want it. . . .

Lesley Hazleton,
"Hers" column, The New York Times

You can always spot them, even from high up,
the brown bulged out trying to make a circle
of a square, the green square inside the brown,
inside the green the brown circle you know is mound
and the big outside green rounded off by a round line
you know is fence. And no one playing.

You've played on everyone. Second base somewhere
on the Dallas Tucson run, New Mexico you think,
where green was brown. Right field outside Chicago
where the fans went silent when you tripled home
the run that beat their best, their all-season
undefeated home town Sox. What a game you pitched
that hot day in the Bronx. You lost to that left hander,
Ford, who made it big, one-nothing on a fluke.
Who's to believe it now? Fat. Bald. Smoking your fear
of the turbulent air you are flying, remembering
the war, a worse fear, the jolting flak, the prayer.

When air settles, the white beneath you opens
and far below in some unpopulated region
of whatever state you are over (it can't be Idaho,
that was years ago) you spot a tiny diamond,
and because you've grown far sighted with age
you see players moving, the center fielder
running the ball down deep, two runners
rounding third, the third base coach waving hard
and the hitter on his own not slowing down
at second, his lungs filled with the cheers of those
he has loved forever, on his magnificent tiny way
to an easy stand-up three.

Richard Hugo,
"From Altitude, the Diamonds"

Marilyn Bridges
Playing Baseball, Allens Creek, NY,
(Detail) 1986
Photograph

The ballpark is the star. In the age of Tris Speaker and Babe Ruth, the era of Jimmie Foxx and Ted Williams, through the empty-seats epoch of Don Buddin and Willie Tasby and unto the decades of Carl Yastrzemski and Jim Rice, the ballpark is the star.

Martin F. Nolan, from
"Fenway: From Frazee to Fisk"

Buzz Spector
Comiskey Park, 1985
Pastel and paper relief

Raoul Dufy
Ball Park—Boston, c. 1950
Watercolor

Tina Chaden
The Baseball Fan, 1985
Paper, clay, and egg tempera

The Sox were playing the Yankees at night and I had a pair of tickets for me and Susan. Box seats.

"Didn't you do some work for this team 10 years ago?" Susan said.

"1975," I said. "The last time they won the pennant."

"That means they finished in first place," Susan said.

"Sort of," I said.

We were walking up Brookline Ave. from Kenmore Square, holding hands, moving with the crowd. Along the way, people offered to sell us Red Sox hats and Red Sox pennants and miniature bats and peanuts and Italian sausages grilled over little charcoal fires. The scent of burning fat was strong in the evening air.

"People are eating those," Susan said.

"Red Sox fans have little regard for personal safety," I said.

"But are they suicidal?" Susan said.

"Often."

We turned into Yawkey Way. And there we were. In front of Fenway: outside the ballpark in the dwindling afternoon, the lights already on inside, tickets purchased, seats reserved, the ballgame in an hour. Outside there were fathers and sons, and overweight women in plastic mesh baseball hats, and scalpers, and pods of young white guys already half gassed, and a couple of old cops with sunburned arms. Inside was eternity. Through the darkness under the stands and up and into the bright green park, bathed in light, changeless and symmetrical, contained, exact, and endlessly different, like water in a stream.

Robert Parker, from
"Spenser's a Fan, Too"

As I look around the empty park, almost Greek in
its starkness, I feel an awesome inarticulate love for
this very stadium and the game it represents. I am
reminded of the story about the baseball fans of
Milwaukee, and what they did on a warm fall
afternoon, the day after it was announced that
Milwaukee was to have a major-league team the next
season. According to the story, 10,000 people went
to County Stadium that afternoon and sat in the
seats and smiled out at the empty playing field—sat
in silence, in awe, in wonder, in anticipation, in joy
—just knowing that soon the field would come alive
with the chatter of infielders, bright as bird chirps.

W. P. Kinsella, from
Shoeless Joe

Jim Dow

County Stadium,
Milwaukee, 1982
Color coupler prints (3)

Vincent Scilla

Spring Training in the
Mountains, 1985
Oil on canvas

Charles Garabedian

Baseball, 1965

Flo-paque on paper

There is no other place as green as this.
I watch the sun go down on the church's steeple.
Overhead the planes make their silent approach.
I drink and the lights take hold, and cheering.

On Silver nights where I have seen
            Grich and Baylor, Bilko and Easter,
            Freed, Cabell, and Crabtree—
            all playing on the green,
I have wished to be here always, as the night is falling,
            always as the lights make
            the colors richer, deeper.

Some histories of the diamond are purely personal:
I sit along the third base line, drink Miller
            or Jenny or Jenny Cream,
eat peanuts, sometimes.
There was a year when no pro ball was played in Rochester.
            I wrote it down.
They raced bicycles that year, while Rochester's team
            played in Montreal.
And some histories, silver with night fall.

Sitting here and keeping score, eyeing the yellow-
            gold of the French's Mustard sign,
watching the kids who hope for the bigs,
there is nothing more on all the silver nights of
            all my summers, nothing more
            that I could wish.
There is no other place in all the world as green as this.

James S. LaVilla-Havelin,
"Silver Nights" .

Jim Dow

Durham Bulls Ballpark, 1981

Color coupler prints (3)

"Chaney Field . . . Home of the Waldorf Little League . . . Enjoy Coca-Cola" proclaim signs at the entrance to the five small baseball fields with a dirt parking lot in their midst.

This is baseball at the bottom line—simple, unadorned, economical, every penny counted, but perfectly satisfactory. If you're a kid and you want to play baseball, here it is. But no come-on, no frills.

A foul ball can reach the railroad tracks. A forest of electrical transformers—the town's power source—looms above the old trees.

The infields are hard, baked dirt full of pebbles, but no rocks or glass. The outfields are splotchy grass, but green. The waist-high cyclone fences surrounding the fields have no fancy distance markers. There are no lights. Get finished by sundown.

The chalk scoreboards aren't used. The bleachers are half-full when they hold a dozen parents. This is word-of-mouth baseball.

"What inning is it? . . . What's the score? . . . Who's winning?" a player asks his mother in quick succession.

And he's the pitcher.

"Coach," pleads an eleven-year-old whose back is barely big enough to contain the uniform words Ken Dixon Chevrolet-Buick-Honda, "somebody's got to help me. Scott just filled my batting helmet with dirt."

This is partly baseball, but mostly growing up, mostly one of those few remaining places where everybody gathers to pass on the tribe's collective sense of itself.

Thomas Boswell, *from*
How Life Imitates the World Series

Walter Iooss, Jr.
Little League, East Orange, NJ, 1965
Photograph

Ralph Fasanella
Sandlot Game (Detail), 1954
Oil on canvas

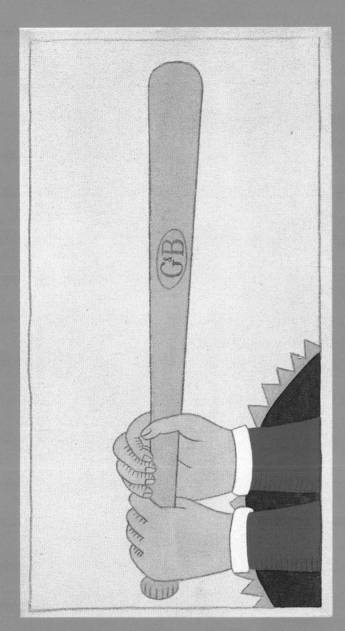

Jim Markowich and Paul Kuhrman
The Ace of Bats (from the Tarot
   de Cooperstown), 1983
Acrylic and colored pencil on canvas

A Louisville Slugger;
a baseball, that perfect object
for a man's hand; the smell of
varnish and leather; and a well-
worn and well-used, older
brother's glove.

James Sullivan
Game Ball, 1987
Charcoal on paper

It weighs just over five ounces and measures between 2.86 and 2.94 inches in diameter. It is made of a composition-cork nucleus encased in two thin layers of rubber, one black and one red, surrounded by 121 yards of tightly wrapped blue-gray wool yarn, 45 yards of white wool yarn, 53 more yards of blue-gray wool yarn, 150 yards of fine cotton yarn, a coat of rubber cement, and a cowhide (formerly horsehide) exterior, which is held together with 216 slightly raised red cotton stitches. Printed certifications, endorsements, and outdoor advertising spherically attest to its authenticity. Like most institutions, it is considered inferior in its present form to its ancient archetypes, and in this case the complaint is probably justified; on occasion in recent years it has actually been known to come apart under the demands of its brief but rigorous active career. Baseballs are assembled and handstitched in Taiwan (before this year the work was done in Haiti, and before 1973 in Chicopee, Massachusetts), and contemporary pitchers claim that there is a tangible variation in the size and feel of the balls that now come into play in a single game; a true peewee is treasured by hurlers, and its departure from the premises, by fair means or foul, is secretly mourned. But never mind: any baseball is beautiful. No other small package comes as close to the ideal in design and utility. It is a perfect object for a man's hand. Pick it up and it instantly suggests its purpose; it is meant to be thrown a considerable distance—thrown hard and with precision. Its feel and heft are the beginning of the sport's critical dimensions; if it were a fraction of an inch

Michael Langenstein
Play Ball, 1982
Postcard collage

larger or smaller, a few centigrams heavier or lighter, the game of baseball would be utterly different. Hold a baseball in your hand. As it happens, this one is not brand new. Here, just to one side of the curved surgical welt of stitches, there is a pale-green grass smudge, darkening on one edge almost to black—the mark of an old infield play, a tough grounder now lost in memory. Feel the ball, turn it over in your hand; hold it across the seam or the other way, with the seam just to the side of your middle finger. Speculation stirs. You want to get outdoors and throw this spare and sensual object to somebody or, at the very least, watch somebody else throw it. The game has begun.

Roger Angell, *from*
Five Seasons

Jed Devine
Untitled, 1985
Palladium print

When Francis opened the trunk lid the odor of lost time filled the attic air, a cloying reek of imprisoned flowers that unsettled the dust and fluttered the window shades. Francis felt drugged by the scent of the reconstituted past, and then stunned by his first look inside the trunk, for there, staring out from a photo, was his own face at age nineteen. The picture lay among rolled socks and a small American flag, a Washington Senators cap, a pile of newspaper clippings and other photos, all in a scatter on the trunk's tray. Francis stared up at himself from the bleachers in Chadwick Park on a day in 1899, his face unlined, his teeth all there, his collar open, his hair unruly in the afternoon's breeze. He lifted the picture for a closer look and saw himself among a group of men, tossing a baseball from bare right hand to gloved left hand. The flight of the ball had always made this photo mysterious to Francis, for the camera had caught the ball clutched in one hand and also in flight, arcing in a blur toward the glove. What the camera had caught was two instants in one: time separated and unified, the ball in two places at once, an eventuation as inexplicable as the Trinity itself. Francis now took the picture to be a Trinitarian talisman (a hand, a glove, a ball) for achieving the impossible: for he had always believed it impossible for him, ravaged man, failed human, to reenter history under this roof. Yet here he was in this aerie of reconstitutable time, touching untouchable artifacts of a self that did not yet know it was ruined, just as the ball, in its inanimate ignorance, did not know yet that it was going nowhere, was caught.

And Francis is not yet ruined, except as an apparency in process.

The ball still flies.

Francis still lives to play another day. Doesn't he?

William Kennedy, *from*
Ironweed

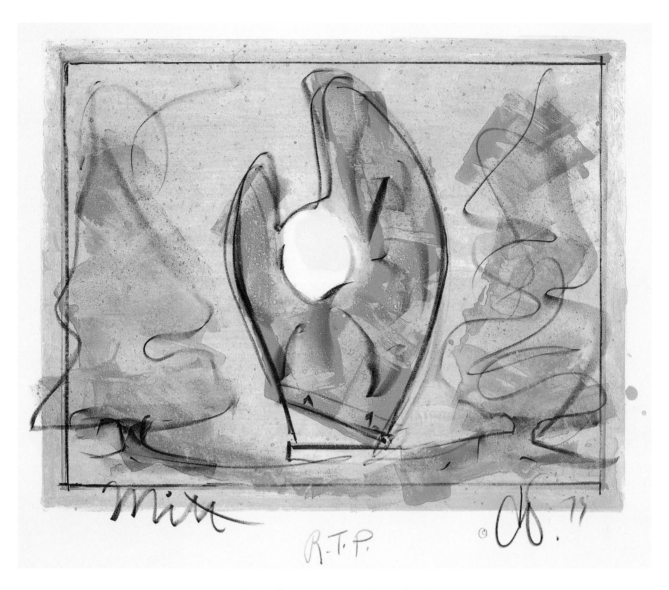

Claes Oldenburg
Mitt, 1973
Lithograph

The ball comes up too fast—hard spot—
and kisses leather on leather a quick goodbye,
only to roll dead in the left field grass.
I can just stare at that spot
where the ball swift-lipped the basepath dirt aside.
The crowd is not loud. In fact, I hardly hear it
so far away, with the winning run touched to plate
and my team slowly going, still floating past.
Slight sounds of mouths, fists punching at pockets
wishing for that ball—Why wasn't it to mine?
A hand lightly slaps my shoulder. Most words
are probably all the same. Dead. So I turn
and watch that ball, fallen in the autumn sun.
At dusk I throw my glove, throw it down
twice. That shiny spot stays there still.

Paul Weinman,
"Where It Had Been Oiled"

Ever since the first caveman picked up the first cudgel, went to his front door and smacked the first nosy saber-toothed tiger in the snout, mankind has known the atavistic power and pleasure of the bat.

From Robin Hood's quarterstaff to Paul Bunyan's ax, men of myth have loved the taper of a handle, the texture of wood grain, the centrifugal surge in the end of a whirling mass. Axes and stout staves have dwindled in everyday use. Now, that ancient inherited desire for thudding force, for an instrument that will deliver a satisfying blow, has descended to the baseball bat.

Thomas Boswell, *from*
How Life Imitates the World Series

Scott Mlyn
Ron Cey, Wrigley Field,
   Chicago, 1986
Photograph

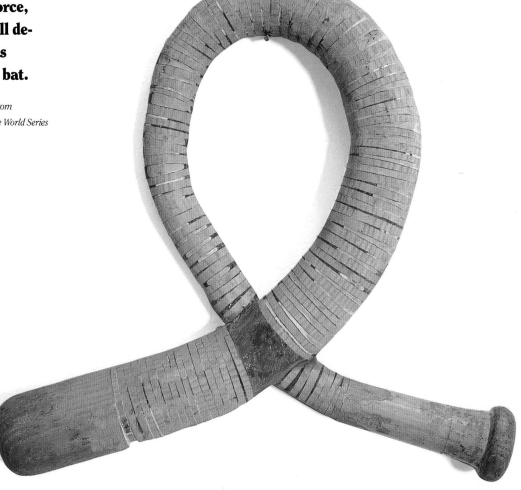

Margaret Wharton
Bat-e, 1985
Wood and epoxy

At the newspaper where I work we have a rule that staff members are not allowed to accept any gift of significant value from an outside source. The rule probably makes sense; its purpose is to prevent potential news sources from trying to influence news coverage through the bestowing of lavish presents.

But I recently received something in the mail from an outside company, and if the newspaper makes me give it back they're going to have to drag me out of here kicking and screaming and holding onto it for dear life.

The package was long and narrow. I opened it. Inside was something that brought tears to my eyes and a funny feeling to my throat:

A Louisville Slugger baseball bat—a Bob Greene autographed model.

For five minutes I sat there looking at it and caressing it and speaking softly to it.

There, in the middle of the barrel, was the Louisville Slugger logo, and the famous copyrighted slogan: "Powerized." There, next to the logo, was the trademark of the Hillerich & Bradsby Co., which manufactures Louisville Sluggers.

And there—right at the end of the barrel—were the words PERSONAL MODEL—LOUISVILLE SLUGGER. And where Mickey Mantle's or Hank Aaron's auto-

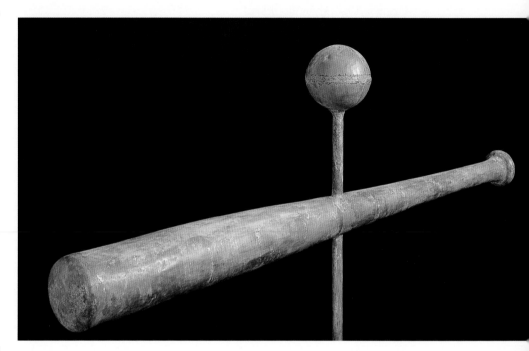

graph ought to be, the script words "Bob Greene."

I suppose there must be some item that an American boy might treasure more fiercely than a Louisville Slugger with his own signature on it, but I can't think of one. For all of us who grew up on sandlots and playgrounds, gripping Louisville Sluggers bearing the autographs of major league stars, the thought of owning one with our own name on the barrel is almost too much to comprehend.

In the box with the Louisville Slugger was a letter from John A. Hillerich III, president of Hillerich & Bradsby. In the letter Hillerich said that this is the centennial

year for Louisville Sluggers; the first one was manufactured in the spring of 1884. Thus, the enclosed bat—a memento of the 100th anniversary.

When I started to show my new bat to people, the response I got was interesting. Women seemed not to care too much; generally they said something like, "Oh, a baseball bat." They would inspect it a little more closely, and then say, "What's your name doing on it?"

But men—men were a different story. First they would see the bat.

Rupert Deese

Whiteness of the Whale, 1984

Oil on canvas

Anonymous

Weathervane, no date

Copper

They'd say something like, "A real Louisville Slugger. That's great." Invariably they would lift it up and go into a batting stance—perhaps for the first time in twenty or thirty years. Then they would roll the bat around in their hands— and finally they would see the signature.

That's when they'd get faint in the head. They would look as if they were about to swoon. Their eyes would start to resemble pin-wheels. And in reverential whispers, they would say: "That is the most wonderful thing I have ever seen. Your own name on a Louisville Slugger. You are so lucky."

For it is true: a Louisville Slugger, for the American male, is a talisman—a piece of property that carries such symbolic weight and meaning that words of description do not do it justice. I have a friend who has two photographs mounted above his desk at work. One photo shows Elvis Presley kissing a woman. The other shows Ted Williams kissing his Louisville Slugger. No one ever asks my friend the meaning of those pictures; the meaning, of course, is quite clear without any explanation.

Hillerich & Bradsby has a photo in its archives that is similarly moving. In the photo, Babe Ruth and Lou Gehrig are standing in a batting cage. Gehrig, a wide smile on his face, is examining the bat. Perhaps you could find another photo that contains three figures more holy to the American male than those three—Ruth, Gehrig, and a Louisville Slugger—but I don't know where you'd look.

Hillerich & Bradsby has some intriguing figures and facts about Louisville Sluggers. The company manufactures approximately one million of them each year. That requires the use of about two hundred thousand trees each baseball season; the company

Claes Oldenburg

Bat Spinning at the Speed of Light, 1975
Lithograph

The Equipment

owns five thousand acres of timberland in Pennsylvania and New York to provide the trees. Ash timber is the wood of choice for Louisville Sluggers. Years ago, the wood of choice was hickory.

According to the company, a professional baseball player uses an average of seventy-two bats each season—which comes as a surprise to those of us who always envisioned a major leaguer using the same special good-luck bat for years on end. The company says that, during World War II, some American sporting goods found their way to a German prison camp in Upper Silesia; the American prisoners of war there reportedly cried at the sight of the Louisville Sluggers. During the Korean War, an American soldier reportedly dashed out of his trench during a firefight to retrieve a Louisville Slugger he had left out in the open before the battle began.

As I sit here typing this, a colleague—a male—has just walked up next to my computer terminal, lifted my Louisville Slugger to his shoulder, and gone into a batter's crouch. In a moment, if I'm right, he'll start examining the bat—and in another moment he'll see the autograph.

I can't wait.

Bob Green,
"Louisville Slugger"

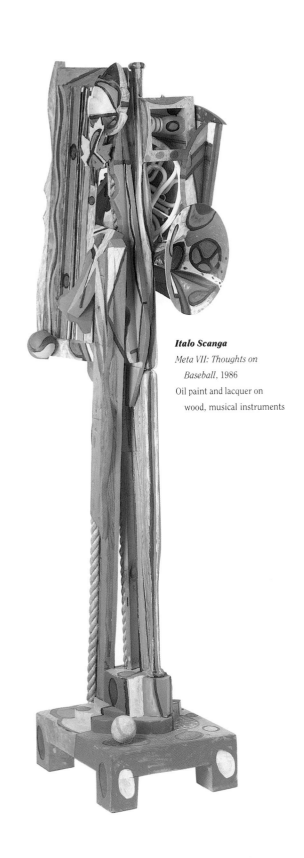

Gerry Bergstein
My Turn at Bat, 1987
Oil on canvas

Italo Scanga
Meta VII: Thoughts on Baseball, 1986
Oil paint and lacquer on wood, musical instruments

Jim Markowich and Paul Kuhrman
The Ace of Bases (from the Tarot de Cooperstown), 1983
Acrylic and colored pencil on canvas

**[I] retrace by moonlight the roads where
I used to play in the sun.** —Marcel Proust

At night, when I go out to the field
to listen to the birds sleep, the stars
hover like old umpires over the diamond,
and I think back upon the convergences
of bats and balls, of cowhide and the whacked
thumping of cork into its oiled pockets,
and I realize again that our lives pass
like the phased signals of that old coach,
the moon, passing over the pitcher's mound,
like the slowed stride of an aging shortstop
as he lopes over the infield or the stilled echo
of crowds in a wintered stadium. I see again
how all the old heroes have passed on to their
ranches and dealerships, that each new season
ushers in its crop of the promised and promising,
the highly touted and the sudden phenoms of the
unexpected, as if the hailed dispensation of gifts
had realigned itself into a new constellation,
as if the old passages of decrepitude and promise
had been altered into a new seeming. I remember
how once, sliding into second during a steal,
I watched the sun rest like a diadem against the
head of some spectator, and thought to myself
in the neat preutterance of all true feeling,
how even our thieveries, well-done, are blessed
with a certain luminousness, how a man rising

from a pilfered sanctity might still upright himself
and return, like Odysseus, to some plenitude
of feast and fidelity. It is why, even then, I loved
baseball: the fierce legitimacy of the neatly stolen,
the calm and illicit recklessness of the coaches
with their wet palms and arcane tongues of mimicry
and motion. It is why, even now, I steal away
from my wife's warm arms to watch the moon sail
like a well-hit fly over the stadium, then hump
my back high over the pitcher's mound and throw
that old curve of memory toward the plate
where I run for a swing at it—the moon
and the stars approving my middle-aged bravado,
that boy still rising from his theft to find the light.

Michael Blumenthal,
"Night Baseball"

David Burnett
Pre-game in the Sally League, 1981
Photograph

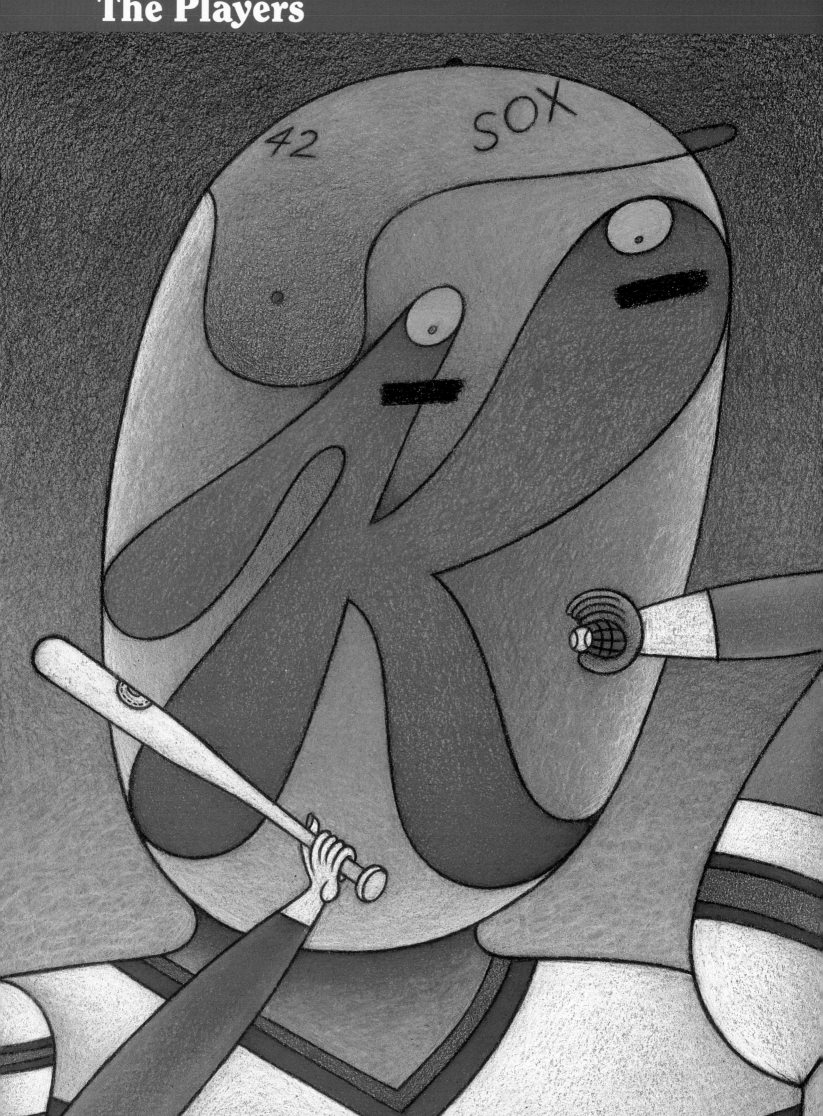

Nickolas Muray
Babe Ruth, c. 1938
Photograph

The heroes and the
has-beens; the great memorable
teams and those frustrating
perennial losers; and the
daydream of making that
impossible catch.

Jim Nutt
Ron Kittle, 1985
Colored pencil on paper

Stephen Shore
Graig Nettles, Fort Lauderdale
Yankee Stadium, Fort
Lauderdale, Florida, 1978
Photograph

Fenway Park, in Boston, is a lyric little bandbox of a ballpark. Everything is painted green and seems in curiously sharp focus, like the inside of an old-fashioned peeping-type Easter egg. It was built in 1912 and rebuilt in 1934, and offers, as do most Boston artifacts, a compromise between Man's Euclidean determinations and Nature's beguiling irregularities. Its right field is one of the deepest in the American League, while its left field is the shortest; the high left-field wall, three hundred and fifteen feet from home plate along the foul line, virtually thrusts its surface at right-handed hitters. On the afternoon of Wednesday, September 28th, 1960, as I took a seat behind third base, a uniformed groundkeeper was treading the top of this wall, picking batting-practice home runs out of the screen, like a mushroom gatherer seen in Wordsworthian perspective on the verge of a cliff. The day was overcast, chill, and uninspirational. The Boston team was the worst in twenty-seven seasons. A jangling medley of incompetent youth and aging competence, the Red Sox were finishing in seventh place only because the Kansas City Athletics had locked them out of the cellar. They were scheduled to play the Baltimore Orioles, a much nimbler blend of May and December, who had been dumped from pennant contention a week before by the insatiable Yankees. I, and 10,453 others, had shown up primarily because this was the Red Sox's last home game of the season, and therefore the last time in all eternity that their regular left fielder, known to the headlines as TED, KID, SPLINTER, THUMPER, TW, and, most cloyingly, misTer Wonderful, would play in Boston. "WHAT WILL WE DO WITHOUT TED? HUB FANS ASK" ran the headline on a newspaper being read by a bulb-nosed cigar smoker a few rows away. Williams' retirement had been announced, doubted (he had been threatening retirement for years), confirmed by Tom Yawkey, the Red Sox owner, and at last widely accepted as the sad but probable truth. He was forty-two and had redeemed his abysmal season of 1959 with a—considering his advanced age—fine one. He had been giving away his gloves and bats and had grudgingly consented to a sentimental ceremony today. This was not necessarily his last game; the Red Sox were scheduled to travel to New York and wind up the season with three games there.

I arrived early. The Orioles were hitting fungos on the field. The day before, they had spitefully smothered the Red Sox, 17-4, and neither their faces nor their drab gray visiting-team uniforms seemed very gracious. I wondered who had invited them to the party. Between our heads and the lowering clouds a frenzied organ was thundering through, with an appositeness perhaps accidental, "You *maaaade* me love you, I didn't wanna do it, I didn't wanna do it. . . ."

The affair between Boston and Ted Williams was no mere summer romance; it was a marriage composed of spats, mutual disappointments, and, toward the end, a mellowing hoard of shared memories. It fell into three stages, which may be termed Youth, Maturity, and Age; or Thesis, Antithesis, and Synthesis; or Jason, Achilles, and Nestor.

First there was the by now legendary epoch when the young bridegroom came out of the West and announced "All I want out of life is that when I walk down the street folks will say 'There goes the greatest hitter who ever lived.'" The dowagers of local journalism attempted to give elementary deportment lessons to this child who spake as a god, and to their horror were themselves rebuked. Thus began the long exchange of backbiting, bat-flipping, booing, and spitting that has distinguished Williams' public relations. The spitting incidents of 1957 and 1958 and the similar dockside courtesies that Williams has now and then extended to the

grandstand should be judged against this background: the left-field stands at Fenway for twenty years have held a large number of customers who have bought their way in primarily for the privilege of showering abuse on Williams. Greatness necessarily attracts debunkers, but in Williams' case the hostility has been systematic and unappeasable. His basic offense against the fans has been to wish that they weren't there. Seeking a perfectionist's vacuum, he has quixotically desired to sever the game from the ground of paid spectatorship and publicity that supports it. Hence his refusal to tip his cap to the crowd or turn the other cheek to newsmen. It has been a costly theory—it has probably cost him, among other evidences of good will, two Most Valuable Player awards, which are voted by reporters—but he has held to it. While his critics, oral and literary, remained beyond the reach of his discipline, the opposing pitchers were accessible, and he spanked them to the tune of .406 in 1941. He slumped to .356 in 1942 and went off to war.

In 1946, Williams returned from three years as a Marine pilot to the second of his baseball avatars, that of Achilles, the hero of incomparable prowess and beauty who nevertheless was to be found sulking in his tent while the Trojans (mostly Yankees) fought

through to the ships. Yawkey, a timber and mining maharajah, had surrounded his central jewel with many gems of slightly lesser water, such as Bobby Doeer, Dom DiMaggio, Rudy York, Birdie Tebbetts, and Johnny Pesky. Throughout the late forties, the Red Sox were the best paper team in baseball, yet they had little three-dimensional to show for it, and if this was a tragedy, Williams was Hamlet. A succinct review of the indictment—and a fair sample of appreciative sports-page prose —appeared the very day of Williams' valedictory, in a column by Huck Finnegan in the Boston *American* (no sentimentalist, Huck):

"Williams' career, in contrast [to Babe Ruth's], has been a series of failures except for his averages. He flopped in the only World Series he ever played in (1946) when he batted only .200. He flopped in the playoff game with Cleveland in 1948. He flopped in the final game of the 1949 season with the pennant hinging on the outcome (Yanks 5, Sox 3). He flopped in 1950 when he returned to the lineup after a two-month absence and ruined the morale of a club that seemed pennant-bound under Steve O'Neill. It has always been Williams' records first, the team second, and the Sox nonwinning record is proof enough of that."

There are answers to all this, of course. The fatal weakness of the great Sox slugging teams was not-quite-good-enough pitching rather than Williams' failure to hit a home run every time he came to bat. Again, Williams' depressing effect on his teammates has never been proved. Despite ample coaching to the contrary, most insisted that they *liked* him. He has been generous with advice to any player who asked for it. In an increasingly combative baseball atmosphere, he continued to duck beanballs docilely. With umpires he was gracious to a fault. This courtesy itself annoyed his critics, whom there was no pleasing. And against the ten crucial games (the seven World Series games with the St. Louis Cardinals, the 1948 playoff with the Cleveland Indians, and the two-game series with the Yankees at the end of the 1949 season, when one victory would have given the Red Sox the pennant) that make up the Achilles' heel of Williams' record, a mass of statistics can be set showing that day in and day out he was no slouch in the clutch. The correspondence columns of the Boston papers now and then suffer a sharp flurry of arithmetic on this score; indeed, for Williams to have distributed all his hits so they did nobody else any good would constitute a feat of placement unparalleled in the annals of selfishness.

Whatever residue of truth remains of the Finnegan charge those of us who love Williams must transmute as best we can, in our own personal crucibles. My personal memories of Williams began when I was a boy in Pennsylvania, with two last-place teams in Philadelphia to keep me company. For me, "W'ms, lf" was a figment of the box scores who always seemed to be going 3-for-5. He radiated, from afar, the hard blue glow of high purpose. I remember listening over the radio to the All-Star Game of 1946, in which Williams hit two singles and two home runs, the second one off a Rip Sewell "blooper" pitch; it was like hitting a balloon out of the park. I remember watching one of his home runs from the bleachers of Shibe Park; it went over the first baseman's head and rose methodically along a straight line and was still rising when it cleared the fence. The trajectory seemed qualitatively different from anything anyone else might hit. For me, Williams is the classic ballplayer of the game on a hot August weekday, before a small crowd, when the only thing at stake is the tissue-thin difference between a thing done well and a thing done ill. Baseball is a game of the long season, of relentless and gradual averaging-out. Irrelevance—since the reference point of most individual contests is remote and statistical—always threatens its interest, which can be maintained not by the occasional heroics that sportswriters feed upon but by players who always *care*; who care, that is to say, about themselves and their art. Insofar as the clutch hitter is not a sportswriter's myth, he is a vulgarity, like a writer who writes only for money. It may be that, compared to such manager's dreams as the manifestly classy Joe DiMaggio and the always helpful Stan Musial, Williams was an icy star. But of all team sports, baseball, with its graceful intermittences of action, its immense and tranquil field sparsely settled with poised men in white, its dispassionate mathematics, seems to me best suited to accommodate, and be ornamented by, a loner. It is an essentially lonely game. No other player visible to my generation concentrated within himself so much of the sport's poignance, so assiduously refined his natural skills, so constantly brought to the plate that intensity of competence that crowds the throat with joy.

By the time I went to college, near Boston, the lesser stars Yawkey had assembled around Williams had faded, and his rigorous pride of craftsmanship had become itself a kind of hero-

ism. This brittle and tempera-
mental player developed an unexpected quality of persistence. He
was always coming back—back
from Korea, back from a broken
collarbone, a shattered elbow, a
bruised heel, back from drastic
bouts of flu and ptomaine poison-
ing. Hardly a season went by
without some enfeebling mishap,
yet he always came back, and always looked like himself. The
delicate mechanism of timing and
power seemed sealed, shockproof,
in some case deep within his
frame. In addition to injuries,
there was a heavily publicized di-
vorce, and the usual storms with
the press, and the Williams Shift
—the maneuver, custom-built by
Lou Boudreau of the Cleveland Indians, whereby three infielders
were concentrated on the right
side of the infield. Williams could
easily have learned to punch singles through the vacancy on his
left and fattened his average
hugely. This was what Ty Cobb,
the Einstein of average, told him
to do. But the game had changed
since Cobb; Williams believed that
his value to the club and to the
league was as a slugger, so he
went on pulling the ball, trying to
blast it through three men, and
paid the price of perhaps fifteen
points of lifetime average. Like
Ruth before him, he bought the
occasional home run at the cost of
many directed singles—a calcu-

lated sacrifice certainly not, in the
case of a hitter as average-minded
as Williams, entirely selfish.

After a prime so harassed and
hobbled, Williams was granted by
the relenting fates a golden twilight. He became at the end of his
career perhaps the best *old* hitter
of the century. The dividing line
falls between the 1956 and the
1957 seasons. In September of the
first year, he and Mickey Mantle
were contending for the batting
championship. Both were hitting
around .350, and there was no
one else near them. The season
ended with a three-game series
between the Yankees and the Sox,
and, living in New York then, I
went up to the Stadium. Williams
was slightly shy of the four hundred at-bats needed to qualify; the
fear was expressed that the Yankee
pitchers would walk him to pro-
tect Mantle. Instead, they pitched
to him. It was wise. He looked
terrible at the plate, tired and dis-
couraged and unconvincing. He
never looked very good to me in
the Stadium. The final outcome
in 1956 was Mantle .353,
Williams .345.

The next year, I moved from
New York to New England, and it
made all the difference. For in
September of 1957, in the same
situation, the story was reversed.
Mantle finally hit .365; it was the
best season of his career. But
Williams, though sick and old,

had run away from him. A bout of
flu had laid him low in September. He emerged from his cave
in the Hotel Somerset haggard
but irresistible; he hit four suc-
cessive pinch-hit home runs. "I
feel terrible," he confessed, "but
every time I take a swing at the
ball it goes out of the park." He
ended the season with thirty-eight
home runs and an average of .388,
the highest in either league since
his own .406, and, coming from a
decrepit man of thirty-nine, an
even more supernal figure. With
eight or so of the "leg hits" that a
younger man would have beaten
out, it would have been .400. And
the next year, Williams, who in
1949 and 1953 had lost batting
championships by decimal whis-
kers to George Kell and Mickey
Vernon, sneaked in behind his
teammate Pete Runnels and
filched his sixth title, a bargain at
.328.

In 1959, it seemed over. The di-
nosaur thrashed around in the
.200 swamp for the first half of the
season, and was even benched
("rested," Manager Mike Higgins
tactfully said). Old foes like the
late Bill Cunningham began to of-
fer batting tips. Cunningham
thought Williams was jiggling his
elbows; in truth, Williams' neck
was so stiff he could hardly turn
his head to look at the pitcher.
When he swung, it looked like a
Calder mobile with one thread

cut; it reminded you that since 1954 Williams' shoulder had been wired together. A solicitous pall settled over the sports pages. In the two decades since Williams had come to Boston, his status had imperceptibly shifted from that of a naughty prodigy to that of a municipal monument. As his shadow in the record books lengthened, the Red Sox teams around him declined, and the entire American League seemed to be losing life and color to the National. The inconsistency of the new superstars—Mantle, Colavito, and Kaline—served to make Williams appear all the more singular. And off the field, his private philanthropy—in particular, his zealous chairmanship of the Jimmy Fund, a charity for children with cancer—gave him a civic presence matched only by that of Richard Cardinal Cushing. In religion, Williams appears to be a humanist, and a selective one at that, but he and the abrasive-voiced Cardinal, when their good works intersect and they appear in the public eye together, make a handsome pair of seraphim.

Humiliated by his '59 season, Williams determined, once more, to come back. I, as a specimen Williams partisan, was both glad and fearful. All baseball fans believe in miracles; the question is, how *many* do you believe in? He looked like a ghost in spring train-

ing. Manager Jurges warned us ahead of time that if Williams didn't come through he would be benched, just like anybody else. As it turned out, it was Jurges who was benched. Williams entered the 1960 season needing eight home runs to have a lifetime total of 500; after one time at bat in Washington, he needed seven. For a stretch, he was hitting a home run every second game that he played. He passed Lou Gehrig's lifetime total, and finished with 521, thirteen behind Jimmy Foxx, who alone stands between Williams and Babe Ruth's unapproachable 714. The summer was a statistician's picnic. His two-thousandth walk came and went, his eighteen-hundredth run batted in, his sixteenth All-Star Game. At one point, he hit a home run off a pitcher, Don Lee, off whose father, Thornton Lee, he had hit a home run a generation before. The only comparable season for a forty-two-year-old man was Ty Cobb's in 1928. Cobb batted .323 and hit one homer. Williams batted .316 but hit twenty-nine homers.

In sum, though generally conceded to be the greatest hitter of his era, he did not establish himself as "the greatest hitter who ever lived." Cobb, for average, and Ruth, for power, remain supreme. Cobb, Rogers Hornsby, Joe Jackson, and Lefty O'Doul, among

players since 1900, have higher lifetime averages than Williams' .344. Unlike Foxx, Gehrig, Hack Wilson, Hank Greenberg, and Ralph Kiner, Williams never came close to matching Babe Ruth's season home-run total of sixty. In the list of major-league batting records, not one is held by Williams. He is second in walks drawn, third in home runs, fifth in lifetime average, sixth in runs batted in, eighth in runs scored and in total bases, fourteenth in doubles, and thirtieth in hits. But if we allow him merely average seasons for the four-plus seasons he lost to two wars, and add another season for the months he lost to injuries, we get a man who in all the power totals would be second, and not a very distant second, to Ruth. And if we further allow that these years would have been not merely average but prime years, if we allow for all the months when Williams was playing in sub-par condition, if we permit his early and later years in baseball to be some sort of index of what the middle years could have been, if we give him a right-field fence that is not, like Fenway's, one of the most distant in the league, and if—the least excusable "if"—we imagine him condescending to outsmart the Williams Shift, we can defensibly assemble, like a colossus induced from the sizable fragments that

Philip Evergood

*The Early Youth of Babe
   Ruth*, c. 1939
Oil on canvas

do remain, a statistical figure not incommensurate with his grandiose ambition. From the statistics that are on the books, a good case can be made that in the combination of power and average Williams is first; nobody else ranks so high in both categories. Finally, there is the witness of the eyes; men whose memories go back to Shoeless Joe Jackson—another unlucky natural—rank him and Williams together as the best-looking hitters they have seen. It was for our last look that ten thousand of us had come.

Two girls, one of them with pert buckteeth and eyes as black as vest buttons, the other with white skin and flesh-colored hair, like an underdeveloped photograph of a redhead, came and sat on my right. On my other side was one of those frowning chestless young-old men who can frequently be seen, often wearing sailor hats, attending ball games alone. He did not once open his program but instead tapped it, rolled up, on his knee as he gave the game his disconsolate attention. A young lady, with freckles and a depressed, dainty nose that by an optical illusion seemed to thrust her lips forward for a kiss, sauntered down into the box seat right behind the roof of the Oriole dugout. She wore a blue coat with a Northeastern University emblem sewed to it. The girls beside me took it into their heads that this was Williams' daughter. She looked too old to me, and why would she be sitting behind the visitors' dugout? On the other hand, from the way she sat there, staring at the sky and French-inhaling, she clearly was *somebody*. Other fans came and eclipsed her from view. The crowd looked less like a weekday ballpark crowd than like the folks you might find in Yellowstone National Park, or emerging from automobiles at the top of scenic Mount Mansfield. There were a lot of competitively well-dressed couples of tourist age, and not a few babes in arms. A row of five seats in front of me was abruptly filled with a woman and four children, the youngest of them two years old, if that. Someday, presumably, he could tell his grandchildren that he saw Williams play. Along with these tots and second-honeymooners, there were Harvard freshmen, giving off that peculiar nervous glow created when a sufficient quantity of insouciance is saturated with enough insecurity; thick-necked Army officers with brass on their shoulders and steel in their stares, pepperings of priests; perfumed bouquets of Roxbury Fabian fans; shiny salesmen from Albany and Fall River; and those gray, hoarse men—taxi drivers, slaughterers, and bartenders—who will continue to click through the turnstiles long after everyone else has deserted to television and tramporamas. Behind me, two young male voices blossomed, cracking a joke about God's five proofs that Thomas Aquinas exists—typical Boston College levity.

The batting cage was trundled away. The Orioles fluttered to the sidelines. Diagonally across the field, by the Red Sox dugout, a cluster of men in overcoats were festering like maggots. I could see a splinter of white uniform, and Williams' head, held at a self-deprecating and evasive tilt. Williams' conversational stance is that of a six-foot-three-inch man under a six-foot ceiling. He moved away to the patter of flash bulbs, and began playing catch with a young Negro outfielder named Willie Tasby. His arm, never very powerful, had grown lax with the years, and his throwing motion was a kind of muscular drawl. To catch the ball, he flicked his glove hand onto his left shoulder (he batted left but threw right, as every schoolboy ought to know) and let the ball plop into it comically. This catch session with Tasby was the only time all afternoon I saw him grin.

A tight little flock of human sparrows who, from the lambent and pampered pink of their faces, could only have been Boston politicians moved toward the plate.

The loudspeakers mammothly coughed as someone huffed on the microphone. The ceremonies began. Curt Gowdy, the Red Sox radio and television announcer, who sounds like everybody's brother-in-law, delivered a brief sermon, taking the two words "pride" and "champion" as his text. It began. "Twenty-one years ago, a skinny kid from San Diego, California . . ." and ended, "I don't think we'll ever see another like him." Robert Tibolt, chairman of the board of the Greater Boston Chamber of Commerce, presented Williams with a big Paul Revere silver bowl. Harry Carlson, a member of the sports committee of the Boston Chamber, gave him

a plaque, whose inscription he did not read in its entirety, out of deference to Williams' distaste for this sort of fuss. Mayor Collins, seated in a wheelchair, presented the Jimmy Fund with a thousand-dollar check.

Then the occasion himself stooped to the microphone, and his voice sounded, after the others, very Californian; it seemed to be coming, excellently amplified, from a great distance, adolescently young and as smooth as a butternut. His thanks for the gifts had not died from our ears before he glided, as if helplessly, into "In spite of all the terrible things that have been said about me by the knights of the keyboard up

there. . . ." He glanced up at the press rows suspended behind home plate. The crowd tittered, appalled. A frightful vision flashed upon me, of the press gallery pelting Williams with erasers, of Williams clambering up the foul screen to slug journalists, of a riot, of Mayor Collins being crushed. ". . . And they *were* terrible things," Williams insisted, with level melancholy, into the mike. "I'd like to forget them, but I can't." He paused, swallowed his memories, and went on, "I want to say that my years in Boston have been the greatest thing in my life." The crowd, like an immense sail going limp in a change of wind, sighed with relief. Taking all the parts himself, Williams then acted out a vivacious little morality drama in which an imaginary tempter came to him at the beginning of his career and said, "Ted, you can play anywhere you like." Leaping nimbly into the role of his younger self (who in biographical actuality had yearned to be a Yankee), Williams gallantly chose Boston over all the other cities, and told us that Tom Yawkey was the greatest owner in baseball and we were the greatest fans. We applauded ourselves lustily. The umpire came out and dusted the plate. The voice of doom announced over the loudspeakers that after Williams' retirement his uniform number,

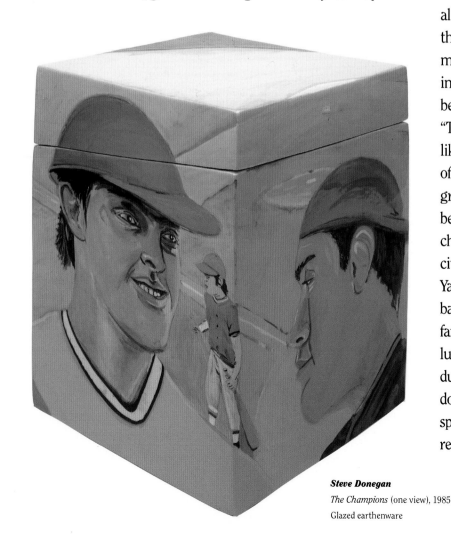

Steve Donegan

The Champions (one view), 1985

Glazed earthenware

9, would be permanently retired—the first time the Red Sox had so honored a player. We cheered. The national anthem was played. We cheered. The game began.

Williams was third in the batting order, so he came up in the bottom of the first inning, and Steve Barber, a young pitcher born two months before Williams began playing in the major leagues, offered him four pitches, at all of which he disdained to swing, since none of them were within the strike zone. This demonstrated simultaneously that Williams' eyes were razor-sharp and that Barber's control wasn't. Shortly, the bases were full, with Williams on second. "Oh, I hope he gets held up at third! That would be wonderful," the girl beside me moaned, and, sure enough, the man at bat walked and Williams was delivered into our foreground. He struck the pose of Donatello's David, the third-base bag being Goliath's head. Fiddling with his cap, swapping small talk with the Oriole third baseman (who seemed delighted to have him drop in), swinging his arms with a sort of prancing nervousness, he looked fine—flexible, hard, and not unbecomingly substantial through the middle. The long neck, the small head, the knickers whose cuffs were worn down near his ankles—all these clichés of sports

Steve Donegan
The Champions (another view), 1985
Glazed earthenware

cartoon iconography were rendered in the flesh.

With each pitch, Williams danced down the baseline, waving his arms and stirring dust, ponderous but menacing, like an attacking goose. It occurred to about a dozen humorists at once to shout "Steal home! Go, go!" Williams' speed afoot was never legendary. Lou Clinton, a young Sox outfielder, hit a fairly deep fly to center field. Williams tagged up and ran home. As he slid across the plate, the ball, thrown with unusual heft by Jackie Brandt, the Oriole center fielder, hit him on the back.

"Boy, he was really loafing, wasn't he?" one of the collegiate

voices behind me said.

"It's cold," the other voice explained. "He doesn't play well when it's cold. He likes heat. He's a hedonist."

The run that Williams scored was the second and last of the inning. Gus Triandos, of the Orioles, quickly evened the score by plunking a home run over the handy left-field wall. Williams, who had had this wall at his back for twenty years, played the ball flawlessly. He didn't budge. He just stood still, in the center of the little patch of grass that his patient footsteps had worn brown, and, limp with lack of interest, watched the ball pass overhead. It was not a very interesting game.

Karl Wirsum

Looking for a Curveball in Cuernavaca, 1983
Acrylic on canvas

Mike Higgins, the Red Sox manager, with nothing to lose, had restricted his major-league players to the left-field line—along with Williams, Frank Malzone, a first-rate third baseman, played the game—and had peopled the rest of the terrain with unpredictable youngsters fresh, or not so fresh, off the farms. Other than Williams' recurrent appearances at the plate, the *maladresse* of the Sox infield was the sole focus of suspense; the second baseman turned every grounder into a juggling act, while the shortstop did a breathtaking impersonation of an open window. With this sort of assistance, the Orioles wheedled their way into a 4-2 lead. They had early replaced Barber with another young pitcher, Jack Fisher. Fortunately (as it turned out), Fisher is no cutie; he is willing to burn the ball through the strike zone, and inning after inning this tactic punctured Higgins' string of test balloons.

Whenever Williams appeared at plate—pounding the dirt from his cleats, gouging a pit in the batter's box with his left foot, wringing resin out of the bat handle with his vehement grip, switching the stick at the pitcher with an electric ferocity—it was like having a familiar Leonardo appear in a shuffle of *Saturday Evening Post* covers. This man, you realized—and here, perhaps, was the difference, greater than the difference in gifts—really desired to hit the ball. In the third inning, he hoisted a high fly to deep center. In the fifth, we thought he had it; he smacked the ball hard and high into the heart of his power zone, but the deep right field in Fenway and the heavy air and a casual east wind defeated him. The ball died. Al Pilarcik leaned his back against the big "380" painted on the right-field wall and caught it. On another day, in another park, it would have been gone. (After the game, Williams said, "I didn't think I could hit one any harder than that. The conditions weren't good.")

The afternoon grew so glowering that in the sixth inning the arc lights were turned on—always a wan sight in the daytime, like the burning headlights of a funeral procession. Aided by the gloom, Fisher was slicing through the Sox rookies, and Williams did not come to bat in the seventh. He was second up in the eighth. This was almost certainly his last time to come to the plate in Fenway Park, and instead of merely cheering, as we had at his three previous appearances, we stood, all of us, and applauded. I had never before heard pure applause in a ballpark. No calling, no whistling, just an ocean of handclaps, minute after minute, burst after burst, crowding and running together in a continuous succession like the pushes of surf at the edge of the sand. It was a sombre and considered tumult. There was not a boo in it. It seemed to renew itself out of a shifting set of memories as the Kid, the Marine, the veteran of feuds and failures and injuries, the friend of children, and the enduring old pro evolved down the bright tunnel of twenty-two summers toward this moment. At last, the umpire signalled for Fisher to pitch; with the other players, he had been frozen in position. Only Williams had moved during the ovation, switching his bat impatiently, ignoring everything except his cherished task. Fisher wound up, and the applause sank into a hush.

Understand that we were a crowd of rational people. We knew that a home run cannot be produced at will; the right pitch must be perfectly met and luck must ride with the ball. Three innings before, we had seen a brave effort fail. The air was soggy, the season was exhausted. Nevertheless, there will always lurk, around the corner in a pocket of our knowledge of the odds, an indefensible hope, and this was one of the times, which you now and then find in sports, when a density of expectation hangs in the air and plucks an event out of the future.

Fisher, after his unsettling wait, was low with the first pitch. He put the second one over, and Williams swung mightily and missed. The crowd grunted, seeing that classic swing, so long and smooth and quick, exposed. Fisher threw the third time, Williams swung again, and there it was. The ball climbed on a diag-onal line into the vast volume of air over center field. From my an-gle, behind third base, the ball seemed less an object in flight than the tip of a towering, mo-tionless construct, like the Eiffel Tower or the Tappan Zee Bridge. It was in the books while it was still in the sky. Brandt ran back to the deepest corner of the outfield grass, the ball descended beyond his reach and struck in the crotch where the bullpen met the wall, bounced chunkily, and vanished.

Like a feather caught in a vortex, Williams ran around the square of bases at the center of our beseeching screaming. He ran as he always ran out home runs—hurriedly, unsmiling, head down, as if our praise were a storm of rain to get out of. He didn't tip his cap. Though we thumped, wept, and chanted "We want Ted" for minutes after he hid in the dugout, he did not come back. Our noise for some seconds passed beyond excitement into a kind of immense open anguish, a wailing, a cry to be saved. But immortality is nontransferable. The papers said that the other players, and even the umpires on the field, begged him to come out and acknowledge us in some way, but he refused. Gods do not answer letters.

Every true story has an anticlimax. The men on the field refused to disappear, as would have seemed decent, in the smoke of Williams' miracle. Fisher continued to pitch, and escaped further harm. At the end of the inning, Higgins sent Williams out to his left-field position, then instantly replaced him with Carrol Hardy, so we had a long last look at Williams as he ran out there and then back, his uniform jobbing, his eyes steadfast on the ground. It was nice, and we were grateful, but it left a funny taste.

One of the scholasticists behind me said, "Let's go. We've seen everything. I don't want to spoil it." This seemed a sound aesthetic decision. Williams' last word had been so exquisitely chosen, such a

perfect fusion of expectation, intention, and execution, that already it felt a little unreal in my head, and I wanted to get out before the castle collapsed. But the game, though played by clumsy midgets under the feeble glow of the arc lights, began to tug at my attention, and I loitered in the runway until it was over. Williams' homer had, quite incidentally, made the score 4-3. In the bottom of the ninth inning, with one out, Marlin Coughtry, the second-base

Nicholas Africano
Ernie Banks (Detail), 1979
Oil, acrylic, wax, and canvas on masonite

juggler, singled. Vic Wertz, pinch-hitting, doubled off the left-field wall, Coughtry advanced to third. Pumpsie Green walked, to load the bases. Willie Tasby hit a double play ball to the third baseman, but in making the pivot throw Billy Klaus, an ex-Red Sox infielder, reverted to form and threw the ball past the first baseman and into the Red Sox dugout. The Sox won, 5-4. On the car radio as I drove home I heard that Williams, his own man to the end, had decided not to accompany the team to New York. He had met the little death that awaits athletes. He had quit.

John Updike,
"Hub Fans Bid Kid Adieu"

"I loved the game," Shoeless Joe went on. "I'd have played for food money. I'd have played free and worked for food. It was the game, the parks, the smells, the sounds. Have you ever held a bat or a baseball to your face? The varnish, the leather. And it was the crowd, the excitement of them rising as one when the ball was hit deep. The sound was like a chorus. Then there was the chug-a-lug of the tin lizzies in the parking lots, and the hotels with their brass spittoons in the lobbies and brass beds in the rooms. It makes me tingle all over like a kid on his way to his first double-header, just to talk about it."

W. P. Kinsella, *from*
Shoeless Joe

Red Grooms
Expos in the Rain, 1985
Gouache on paper (5 sheets)

Scott Mlyn
*Before the Game, Dodger
   Stadium, Los Angeles*, 1985
Photograph

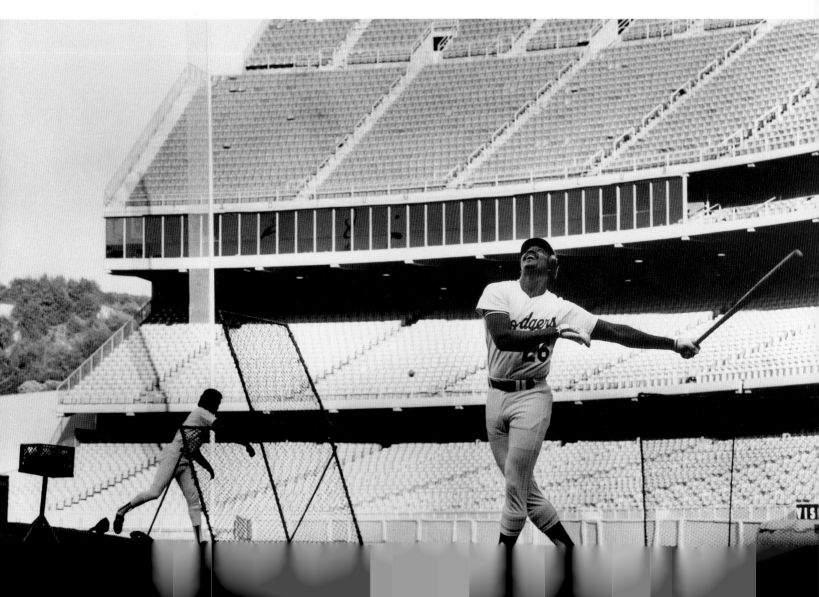

Gerald Garston
Spring Training, 1981
Oil on canvas

Baseball holds so much of the past, pulls me back to it each year, to the soothing unclocked unrolling of the innings, to the sound of an announcer through an open car in May, the sweet attenuations of late summer afternoons, my father bringing us Ted Williams's autograph, my brother, his ear to the radio, suffering a late-season loss. The sound of cleats on an asphalt drive, a bat cracking a ball, delirious cheers for the team that's held me in thrall all my life, the raw power of its line-up, the charisma of the Green Wall. Batting averages, home runs, earned run averages, absorbed unwittingly over the seasons, call out to surprise me in easy conversation with strangers, in a southern city, in a stadium, in spring.

Gail Mazur, from
"Spring Training in the Grapefruit League"

Any man who can look handsome in a dirty baseball suit is an Adonis. There is something about the baggy pants, and the Micawber-shaped collar, and the skull-fitting cap, and the foot or so of tan, or blue, or pink undershirt sleeve sticking out at the arms, that just naturally kills a man's best points. Then too, a baseball suit requires so much in the matter of leg. Therefore, when I say that Rudie Schlachweiler was a dream even in his baseball uniform, with a dirty brown streak right up the side of his pants where he had slid for base, you may know that the girls camped on the grounds during the season.

During the summer months our ball park is to us what the Grand Prix is to Paris, or Ascot is to London. What care we that Evers gets seven thousand a year (or is it a month?); or that Chicago's new South-side ball park seats thirty-five thousand (or is it million?). Of what interest are such meager items compared with the knowledge that "Pug" Coulan, who plays short, goes with Undine Meyers, the girl up there in the eighth row, with the pink dress and the red roses on her hat? When "Pug" snatches a high one out of the firmament we yell with delight, and even as

we yell we turn sideways to look up and see how Undine is taking it. Undine's shining eyes are fixed on "Pug," and he knows it, stoops to brush the dust off his dirt-begrimed baseball pants, takes an attitude of careless grace and misses the next play.

Our grand-stand seats almost two thousand, counting the boxes. But only the snobs, and the girls with new hats, sit in the boxes. Box seats are comfortable, it is true, and they cost only an additional ten cents, but we have come to consider them undemocratic,

Scott Mlyn

Two Fans and Wally Joyner,
  Memorial Stadium, Baltimore, 1986
Photograph

and unworthy of true fans. Mrs. Freddy Van Dyne, who spends her winters in Egypt and her summers at the ball park, comes out to the game every afternoon in her automobile, but she never occupies a box seat; so why should we? She perches up in the grand-stand with the rest of the enthusiasts, and when Kelley puts one over she stands up and clinches her fists, and waves her arms and shouts with the best of 'em.

Edna Ferber, *from*
"Bush League Hero"

There is a diamond chain running from PONY League through Little League to Babe Ruth (which gets you through age 15), and after that, American Legion to 18 or semi-pro where available, and at last some colleges that teach baseball as seriously as they teach football; then on to various degrees of minors and finally the brass ring itself, toward which the whole chain strains; and blessed are those who follow it all the way. Or even part of the way. A guy who's played one game in the pros is like a former State Senator, a big man in most neighborhoods, and any saloon, as long as he lives.

Wilfrid Sheed, *from*
"Diamonds Are Forever,"
The New York Times Magazine

Clyde Singer
Minor League, 1946
Oil on canvas

Sidney Goodman
Tryout, 1965
Oil on canvas

"That's the way it is, Monk. You're good up there as long as you're good. After that they sell you down the river. Hell, I ain't kickin'. I been lucky. I had ten years of it already, an' that's more than most. An' I been in three World's Serious. If I can hold on fer another year or two—if they don't let me go or trade me—I think maybe we'll be in again."

Thomas Wolfe, from
You Can't Go Home Again

They say reflexes, the coach says reflexes, even the papers now are saying reflexes, but I don't think it's the reflexes so much—last night, as a gag to cheer me up, the wife walks into the bedroom wearing one of the kids' rubber gorilla masks and I was under the bed in six-tenths of a second, she had the stopwatch on me. It's that I can't see the ball the way I used to. It used to come floating up with all seven continents showing, and the pitcher's thumbprint, and a grass smooch or two, and the Spalding guarantee in ten-point sans-serif, and *whop*! I could feel the sweet wood with the bat still cocked. Now, I don't know, there's like a cloud around it, a sort of spiral vagueness, maybe the Van Allen belt, or maybe I lift my eye in the last second, planning how I'll round second base, or worrying which I do first, tip my cap or slap the third-base coach's hand. You can't see a blind spot, Kierkegaard says, but in there now, between when the ball leaves the bleacher background and I can hear it plop all fat and satisfied in the catcher's mitt, there's somehow just nothing, where there used to be a lot, everything in fact, because they're not keeping me around for my fielding, and already I see the afternoon tabloid has me down as trade bait.

John Updike, from
"The Slump"

Robert Rauschenberg

Rank, 1964

Lithograph

When Oscar segued perfectly into a second song, his talent seemed awesome to Francis, and the irrelevance of talent to Oscar's broken life even more of a mystery. How does somebody get this good and why doesn't it mean anything? Francis considered his own talent on the ball field of a hazy, sunlit yesterday: how he could follow the line of the ball from every crack of the bat, zap after it like a chicken hawk after a chick, how he would stroke and pocket its speed no matter whether it was lined at him or sizzled erratically toward him through the grass. He would stroke it with the predatory curve of his glove and begin with his right hand even then, whether he was running or falling, to reach into that leather pocket, spear the chick with his educated talons, and whip it across to first or second base, or wherever it needed to go and you're out, man, you're out. No ball player anywhere moved his body any better than Franny Phelan, a damn fieldin' machine, fastest ever was.

Francis remembered the color and shape of his glove, its odor of oil and sweat and leather, and he wondered if Annie had kept it. Apart from his memory and a couple of clippings, it would be all that remained of a spent career that had blossomed and then peaked in the big leagues far too long after the best years were gone, but which brought with the peaking the promise that some belated and overdue glory was possible, that somewhere there was a hosannah to be cried in the name of Francis Phelan, one of the best sonsabitches ever to kick a toe into third base.

William Kennedy, *from*
Ironweed

Michael Hurson
Baseball Player (at bat), 1982
Pencil, pastel, ink, and
conte crayon on paper

Now I feel good when Dave Winfield
throws his bat and it goes spinning
toward the pitcher and looks
intentional to some amateurish to others
but certainly dangerous and loosened
"reckless passionate perhaps innocent"
This was my style
the style of the thrown bat
the style of Ryne Duren
blinded with drink as he later confessed
deranged in all the senses
as he threw balls out of the stadium
behind the batter's head
the impossible pitcher
with an underhand of symbolic force
a pitcher who could only hope
to see the batter
and Reader
I throw my bat at you

David Shapiro,
"Empathy for David Winfield"

Andy Warhol
Pete Rose, 1985
Screenprint

Men on the bases. The crowd, the home crowd, whooping it up. The catcher stood in front of the plate, looking around, hollering orders to the infield, his mask held in his hand. He was fat, and the chest protector made him look fatter. He gestured with the mask to the first baseman and then the third baseman, and they punched their gloves and danced a few steps in response to orders they couldn't possibly hear. It was a good ritual, holding up the game, and the crowd loved it. A fat catcher, when there's no more baseball left in him, can still get by as an actor.

This was the bush. The game was rough and simple, not machine-like, as in the majors. These boys had played baseball since they could walk. Played it until their legs gave out, or they couldn't fight off the extra flesh any more; until their arms turned from rubber to glass. . .

Will was motionless, waiting. The catcher glowered around the infield, then turned toward the mound, and stepped forward. But Will didn't come down to meet him, so he stopped and turned toward the plate. The man in blue, short and stocky, was waiting, jaw thrust forward, hands clasped behind his back. The catcher went back to his position, and the crowd yelled, raucous. He turned to face Will, and put on his mask. Slowly, he let down his weight, went into a crouch, and lifted the bottom flap of the body protector. In front of the gray flannel stretched tight around his bottom, he lowered three fingers, and gave the sign.

Will moved, lifted one leg, drew his feet together. The banks of lights over the first and third base stands flooded directly upon him, and he was aware of the others, over the bleachers, pouring on his back. Shifting his weight to one foot, he began smoothing and re-arranging the loose earth of the mound with the toe cleats of the other. A slow, softshoe dance, with his glove hand on his hip, and his pitching hand holding the ball loosely at his side; his head declined, his figure arrogantly modest and indifferent. A pebble here, a pile of dirt there: building, smoothing, leveling the surface. The earth mound, he thought, surrounded by a forest of grass, the trails through the forest, and beyond, the howling wilds . . . turning, swirling, curving, the toe of the shoe. . . .

James Chapin
Veteran Bush League Catcher, 1948
Oil on canvas

Paul C. Metcalf, *from*
Will West

They cheered and clapped when he and Lucky Ferris came out of the dugout, and when the cheering and clapping settled to sporadic shouts he had already stopped hearing it, because he was feeling the pitches in his right arm and watching them the way he always did in the first few minutes of his warm-up. Some nights the fastball was fat or the curve hung or the ball stayed up around Lucky's head where even the hitters in this Class C league would hit it hard. It was a mystery that frightened him. He threw the first hard one and watched it streak and rise into Lucky's mitt; and the next one; and the next one; then he wasn't watching the ball anymore, as though it had the power to betray him. He wasn't watching anything except Lucky's target, hardly conscious of that either, or of anything else but the rhythm of his high-kicking windup, and the ball not thrown but released out of all his motion; and now he felt himself approaching that moment which he could not achieve alone: a moment that each time was granted to him. Then it came: the ball was part of him, as if his arm stretched sixty feet six inches to Lucky's mitt and slammed the ball into leather and sponge and Lucky's hand. Or he was part of the ball.

Now all he had to do for the rest of the night was concentrate on prolonging that moment. He had trained himself to do that, and while people talked about his speed and curve and change of pace and control, he knew that without his concentration they would be only separate and useless parts; and instead of nineteen and five on the year with an earned run average of two point one five and two hundred and six strikeouts, going for his twentieth win on the last day of the season, his first year in professional ball, three months short of his twentieth birthday, he'd be five and nineteen and on his way home to nothing.

Andre Dubus, *from*
"The Pitcher"

Deryl Daniel Mackie
Smokey Joe Williams, 1985
Acrylic on canvas

"If you're not tired, fish," he said aloud, "you must be very strange."

He felt very tired now and he knew the night would come soon and he tried to think of other things. He thought of the Big Leagues, to him they were the *Gran Ligas*, and he knew that the Yankees of New York were playing the *Tigres* of Detroit.

This is the second day now that I do not know the result of the *juegos*, he thought. But I must have confidence and I must be worthy of the great DiMaggio who does all things perfectly even with the pain of the bone spur in his heel. What is a bone spur? he asked himself. *Un espuela de hueso*. We do not have them. Can it be as painful as the spur of a fighting cock in one's heel? I do not think I could endure that or the loss of the eye and of both eyes and continue to fight as the fighting cocks do. Man is not much beside the great birds and beasts. Still I would rather be that beast down there in the darkness of the sea.

"Unless sharks come," he said aloud. "If sharks come, God pity him and me."

Do you believe the great DiMaggio would stay with a fish as long as I will stay with this one? he thought. I am sure he would and more since he is young and strong. Also his father was a fisherman. But would the bone spur hurt him too much?

"I do not know," he said aloud. "I never had a bone spur."

Ernest Hemingway, *from*
The Old Man and the Sea

Harvey Dinnerstein
The Wide Swing, 1974
Oil on canvas

Things as critical as this, the selection of a favored baseball team, are not, as some suspect, a matter of choice; one does not choose a team as one does not select his own genes. They are confirmed upon you, more than we know an act of heredity.

David Halberstam, from "The Fan Divided"

Robert Gwathmey
World Series, 1958
Oil on canvas

Oh, my teammates! How can I leave them!

Here is Dock, who shakes hands and says with great formality and gentleness that it has been real good to know me and that I should look him up at the ballpark. I start to walk to the car, slogging through the instant mud. Then Luke runs up. One more thing! If he does make it, sometime, would we please write him for tickets? He sure would be pleased to see us again.

And I him, and my father and my son, and my mother's father when the married men played the single men in Wilmot, New Hampshire, and my father's father's father who hit a ball with a stick while he was camped outside Vicksburg in June of 1863, and maybe my son's son's son for baseball is continuous, like nothing else among American things, an endless game of repeated summers, joining the long generations of all the fathers and all the sons.

Donald Hall, from
"Fathers Playing Catch with Sons"

Anonymous
Untitled, no date
Oil on canvas

Justin McCarthy
Yankees Win Series, 4-3, 1952
Watercolor on board

My years with the Dodgers were 1952 and 1953, two seasons in which they lost the World Series to the Yankees. You may glory in a team triumphant, but you fall in love with a team in defeat. Losing after great striving is the story of man, who was born to sorrow, whose sweetest songs tell of saddest thought, and who, if he is a hero, does nothing in life as becomingly as leaving it. A whole country was stirred by the high deeds and thwarted longings of The Duke, Preacher, Pee Wee, Skoonj and the rest. The team was awesomely good and yet defeated. Their skills lifted everyman's spirit and their defeat joined them with everyman's existence, a national team, with a country in thrall, irresistible and unable to beat the Yankees.

Roger Kahn, *from*
The Boys of Summer

Robert Kushner
LA Dodgers, 1978
Watercolor on paper

In 1959 Ike went to South America
　　And I had the report to write
　　And the Dodgers beat the White Sox
　　In the World Series in an upset.
And I coolly watch the television set and smile
　　And say to myself that this is the first World Series
　　I am living through. I am now old enough
　　To understand what is going on and appreciate
　　And live it for my team, the Dodgers.
And after we won I walked around triumphantly
　　And I wore a Los Angeles Dodger baseball cap . . .

David Lehman, *from*
"The Presidential Years"

John Dreyfuss
Pitcher, 1984
Bronze (edition of 12)

Suddenly I remembered a scene in grave detail from the beginning of my baseball time. It is a Sunday afternoon, 1940 probably, or possibly 1941, when the Dodgers will win the pennant and meet the Yankees in the series and I will see the first game. My father and my mother and I are riding in the Studebaker, listening to Red Barber broadcast a crucial game between the Dodgers and the Giants. The Giants are ahead. Now the Dodgers begin to come close—maybe they tie the game; I don't remember the details—and the Giants stop, pause, confer. Then they summon Carl Hubbell from the bullpen.

My father explains how momentous it is that Carl Hubbell should pitch relief. Things have not gone well for him lately. But King Carl is the greatest left-hander of all time, who, in the 1934 All Star game, struck out Babe Ruth, Lou Gehrig, Jimmie Foxx, Al Simmons, and Joe Cronin, all in a row; he's an old screwballer who walks always with his left elbow turned into his ribs, his arm permanently twisted by his best pitch. The great man seldom pitched relief, and now he walked from the bullpen to the pitcher's mound and took his tosses; old man who had pitched since 1928, who couldn't have more than three or four dwindling years left in his arm; old man come in to save the game for his faltering team.

My father's face is tense. He loves the Dodgers and not the Giants, but he loves Carl Hubbell even more. My father is thirty-seven years old in 1940. So is Carl Hubbell.

Then the Dodgers send up a pinch hitter. It is Harold Reese, the baby shortstop, former marbles ("pee-wees") champion of Louisville, Kentucky, fresh from the minor leagues, and fifteen years younger than Hubbell. I sit in the front seat cheering the Dodgers on, hoping against hope, though I realize that the rookie shortstop is "good field no hit."

Pee Wee hits a home run off Carl Hubbell and the Dodgers win.

Sitting there in the front seat, eleven years old, I clap and cheer. Then I hear my father's strange voice. I look across my mother to see his knuckles white on the wheel, his face white, and I hear him saying, "The punk! The punk!" With astonishment and horror, I see that my father is crying.

Donald Hall, from
"Fathers Playing Catch with Sons"

So I ran all right, out of the hospital and up to the play-ground and right out to center field, the position I play for a softball team that wears silky blue-and-gold jackets with the name of the club scrawled in big white felt letters from one shoulder to another: S E A B E E S, A.C. Thank God for the Seabees A.C.! Thank God for center field! Doctor, you can't imagine how truly glorious it is out there, so alone in all that space . . . Do you know baseball at all? Because center field is like some obser-vation post, a kind of control tower, where you are able to see everything and everyone, to un-derstand what's happening the instant it happens, not only by the sound of the struck bat, but by the spark of movement that goes through the infielders in the first second that the ball comes flying at them; and once it gets beyond them, "It's mine," you call, "it's mine," and then after it you go. For in center field, if you can get to it, it *is* yours. Oh, how unlike my home it is to be in center field, where no one will appropriate unto himself anything that I say is *mine*!

Unfortunately, I was too anx-ious a hitter to make the high school team—I swung and missed at bad pitches so often

during the tryouts for the freshman squad that eventually the ironical coach took me aside and said, "Sonny, are you sure you don't wear glasses?" and then sent me on my way. But did I have form! did I have style! And in my playground softball league, where the ball came in just a little slower and a little bigger, I am the star I dreamed I might become for the whole school. Of course, still in my ardent desire to excel I too frequently swing and miss, but when I connect, it goes great distances, Doctor, it flies over fences and is called a home run. Oh, and there is really nothing in life, nothing at all, that quite compares with that pleasure of rounding sec-ond base at a nice slow clip, because there's just no hurry anymore, because that ball you've hit has just gone sailing out of sight . . . And I could field, too, and the farther I had to run, the better. "I got it! I got it! I got it!" and tear in to-ward second, to trap in the webbing of my glove—and barely an inch off the ground— a ball driven hard and low and right down the middle, a base hit, someone thought . . . Or back I go, "*I* got it, I got it—" back easily and gracefully to-ward that wire fence, moving practically in slow motion, and

then that delicious Di Maggio sensation of grabbing it like something heaven-sent over one shoulder . . . Or running! turning! leaping! like little Al Gionfriddo—a baseball player, Doctor, who once did a very great thing . . . Or just standing nice and calm—nothing trem-bling, everything serene— standing there in the sunshine (as though in the middle of an empty field, or passing the time on the street corner), standing without a care in the world in the sunshine, like my king of kings, the Lord My God, The Duke Himself (Snider, Doctor, the name may come up again), standing there as loose and as easy, as happy as I will ever be, just waiting by myself under a high fly ball (*a towering fly ball*, I hear Red Barber say, as he watches from behind his mi-crophone—hit out toward Portnoy; *Alex under it, under it*), just waiting there for the ball to fall into the glove I raise to it, and yup, there it is, *plock*, the third out of the inning (*and Alex gathers it in for out num-ber three, and, folks, here's old C.D. for P. Lorillard and Com-pany*), and then in one motion, while old Connie brings us a message from Old Golds, I start in toward the bench, holding the ball now with the five fin-gers of my bare left hand, and when I get to the infield—having come down hard with one foot on the bag at second base —I shoot it gently, with just a flick of the wrist, at the opposing team's shortstop as he comes trotting out onto the field, and still without breaking stride, go loping in all the way, shoulders shifting, head hanging, a touch pigeon-toed, my knees coming slowly up and down in an altogether brilliant imitation of The Duke. Oh, the unruffled nonchalance of that game! There's not a movement that I don't know still down in the tissue of my muscles and the joints between my bones. How to bend over to pick up my glove and how to toss it away, how to test the weight of the bat, how to hold it and carry it and swing it around in the on-deck circle, how to raise that bat above my head and flex and loosen my shoulders and my neck before stepping in and planting my two feet exactly where my two feet belong in the batter's box—and how, when I take a called strike (which I have a tendency to do, it balances off nicely swinging at bad pitches), to step out and express, if only through a slight poking with the bat at the ground, just the right amount of exasperation with the powers that be . . . yes, every little de-

tail so thoroughly studied and mastered, that it is simply beyond the realm of possibility for any situation to arise in which I do not know how to move, or where to move, or what to say or leave unsaid . . .
And it's true, is it not?
—incredible, but
apparently true
—there are peo-
ple who feel in life the ease, the self-assurance, the simple and essential affiliation with what is going on, that I used to feel as the center fielder for the Seabees? Because it wasn't, you see, that one was the best center fielder imaginable, only that one knew exactly, and down to the smallest particular, how a center fielder should conduct himself. And there are people like that walking the streets of the U.S. of A.? I ask you, why can't I be one! Why can't I exist now as I existed for the Seabees out there in center field! Oh, to be a center fielder, a center fielder—and nothing more!

Philip Roth, *from*
Portnoy's Complaint

William King
Self as Doubleday, 1986
Red vinyl

Dan Rather, fifty-two, is anchor of the "CBS Evening News." "When I was thirteen, I had rheumatic fever," he said. "I became extremely skinny and extremely weak, but I still went out for the seventh-grade baseball team at Alexander Hamilton Junior High School in Houston.

"The school was small enough that there was no cut as such; you were supposed to figure out that you weren't good enough, and quit. Game after game I sat at the end of the bench, hoping that maybe this was the time I would get in. The coach never even looked at me; I might as well have been invisible.

"I told my mother about it. Her advice was not to quit. So I went to practice every day, and I tried to do well so that the coach would be impressed. He never even knew I was there. At home in my room I would fantasize that there was a big game, and the three guys in front of me would all get hurt, and the coach would turn to me and put me in, and I would make the winning hit. But then there'd be another game, and the late innings would come, and if we were way ahead I'd keep hoping that this was the game when the coach would put me in. He never did.

"When you're that age, you're looking for someone to tell you you're okay. Your sense of self-esteem is just being formed. And what that experience that baseball season did was make me think that perhaps I wasn't okay.

"In the last game of the season something terrible happened. It was the last of the ninth inning, there were two outs, and there were two strikes on the batter. And the coach turned to me and told me to go out to right field.

"It was a totally humiliating thing for him to do. For him to put me in for one pitch, the last pitch of the season, in front of all the other guys on the team . . . I stood out there for that one pitch, and I just wanted to sink into the ground and disappear. Looking back on it, it was an extremely unkind thing for him to have done. That was nearly forty years ago, and I don't know why the memory should be so vivid now; I've never known if the coach was purposely making fun of me—and if he was, why a grown man would do that to a thirteen-year-old boy.

"I'm not a psychologist. I don't know if a man can point to one event in his life and say that that's the thing that made him the way he is. But when you're that age, and you're searching for your own identity, and all you want is to be told that you're all right . . . I wish I understood it better, but I know the feeling is still there."

Dan Rather, *quoted by*
Bob Greene, from
"Cut"

We were only farm team
not "good enough" to
make big Little League
with its classic uniforms
deep lettered hats.
But our coach said
we *were* just as good
maybe better
so we played
the Little League champs
in our stenciled tee shirts
and soft purple caps
when the season was over.

What happened that afternoon
I can't remember—
whether we won or tied.
But in my mind I lean back
to a pop-up hanging
in sunny sky
stopped
nailed to the blue
losing itself in a cloud
over second base
where I stood waiting.

Ray Michaud who knew
my up-and-down career
as a local player
my moments of graceful
   genius
my unpredictable ineptness
screamed arrows at me
from the dugout
where he waited to bat:
"He's gonna drop it! He
don't know how to catch,
you watch it drop!"

The ball kept climbing
higher, a black dot
no rules of gravity, no
brakes, a period searching
for a sentence, and the
   sentence read:
"You're no good, Bill
you won't catch this one now
you know you never will."

I watched myself looking up
and felt my body rust, falling
in pieces to the ground
a baby trying to stand up
an ant in the shadow of a house

I wasn't there
had never been born
would stand there forever
a statue squinting upward
pointed out laughed at
for a thousand years
teammates dead, forgotten
bones of anyone who played
   baseball
forgotten
baseball forgotten, played
   no more
played by robots on electric
   fields
who never missed
or cried in their own sweat

I'm thirty-four years old.
The game was over twenty
   years ago.
All I remember of that
   afternoon
when the ball came down

is that
I caught it.

Bill Zavatsky,
"Baseball"

The ball is hit sharply toward me on the ground, and I drift over, sweep down, rise, and a wave of terror rises in my back and I go blind and throw the ball about ten feet over Donnie Leka's head. I watch his head sail helplessly away.

The count is three balls and two strikes. Bases loaded, bottom of the something like seventh. I step out of the box and sneak a look at the pitcher. My insides are trembling. I suddenly realize that he must feel as nervous as I do. No problem: he'll walk me. Called strike three, right down the middle. Tears blur my eyes as I jog over toward the bench to get my glove and go back out to short.

The ball is hit sharply toward me on the ground, and I drift over, sweep down, rise, and a wave of terror rises in my back and I go blind and throw the ball about ten feet over Donnie Leka's head.

Ron Padgett,
"Little League Jinx"

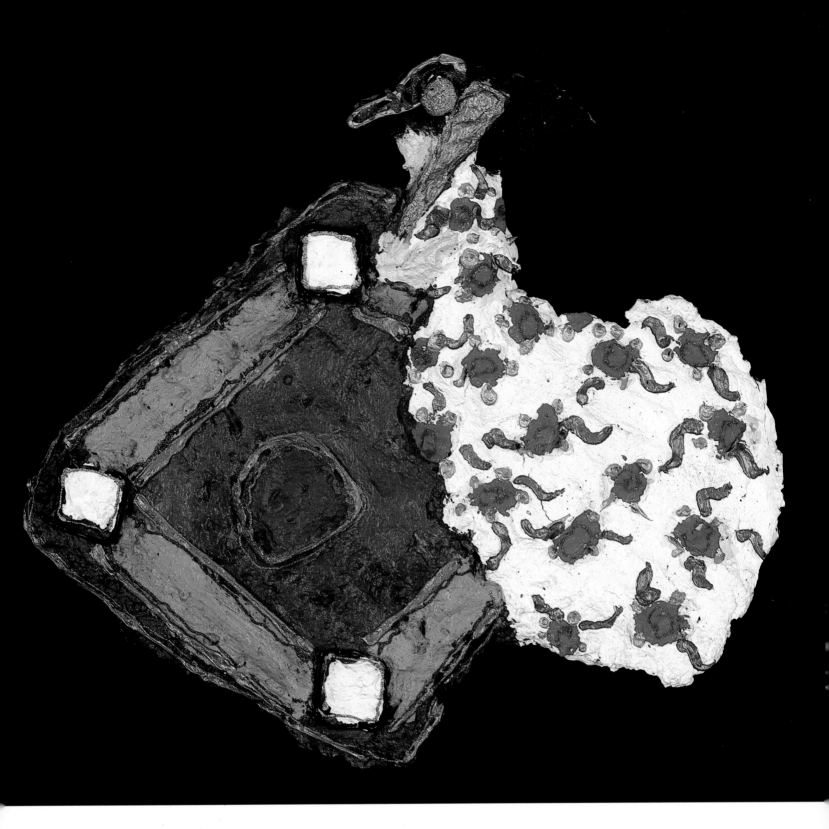

Claudia DeMonte

*Claudia at Doubleday
Field*, 1984
Pulp, paper, acrylic, and
mixed media

Outside on the grass is Eugene Jerome, *almost but not quite fifteen. He is wearing knickers, a shirt and tie, a faded and torn sweater, Keds sneakers and a blue baseball cap. He has a beaten and worn baseball glove on his left hand and in his right hand he holds a ball that is so old and battered, it is ready to fall apart.*

On an imaginary pitcher's mound, facing stage left, he looks back over his shoulder to an imaginary runner on second, then back over to the "batter." Then he winds up and pitches, hitting an offstage wall.

Eugene. One out, a man on second, bottom of the seventh, two balls, no strikes . . . Ruffing checks the runner on second, gets the sign from Dickey, Ruffing stretches, Ruffing pitches: (*He throws the ball.*) Caught the inside corner, steerike one! Atta baby! No hitter up there. (*He retrieves the ball.*) One out, a man on second, bottom of the seventh, two balls one strike . . . Ruffing checks the runner on second, gets the sign from Dickey, Ruffing stretches, Ruffing pitches—(*He throws the ball.*) Low and outside, ball three. Come on, Red! Make him a hitter! No batter up there. In there all the time, Red.

Blanche. (*stops sewing*) Kate, please. My head is splitting.

Kate. I told that boy a hundred and nine times. (*She yells out.*) Eugene! Stop banging the wall!

Eugene. (*Calls out*) In a minute, Ma! This is for the World Series! (*back to his game*) One out, a man on second, bottom of the seventh, three balls, one strike . . . Ruffing stretches, Ruffing pitches—(*He throws the ball.*) Oh, no! High and outside, JoJo Moore walks! First and second and Mel Ott lopes up to the plate . . .

Blanche. (*stops again*) Can't he do that someplace else?

KATE. I'll break his arm, that's where he'll do it. (*She calls out*) Eugene, I'm not going to tell you again. Do you hear me?

EUGENE. It's the last batter, Mom. Mel Ott is up. It's a crucial moment in World Series history.

KATE. Your Aunt Blanche has a splitting headache.

BLANCHE. I don't want him to stop playing. It's just the banging.

LAURIE. (*Looks up from her book*) He always does it when I'm studying. I have a big test in history tomorrow.

EUGENE. One pitch, Mom? I think I can get him to pop up. I have my stuff today.

KATE. Your father will give you plenty of stuff when he comes home! You hear?

EUGENE. Alright! Alright!

KATE. I want you inside *now*! Put out the water glasses.

BLANCHE. I can do that.

KATE. Why? Is his arm broken? (*She yells out again*) And I don't want any back talk, you hear? (*She goes back to kitchen*)

EUGENE. (*Slams ball into his glove angrily. Then he cups his hand, making a megaphone out of it and announces to the grandstands*) . . . "Attention, ladeees and gentlemen! Today's game will be delayed because of my Aunt Blanche's headache . . ."

Neil Simon, from
Brighton Beach Memoirs

EUGENE. . . . One day I'm going to put all this in a book or a play. I'm going to be a writer like Ring Lardner or somebody—that's if things don't work out first with the Yankees, or the Cubs, or the Red Sox, or maybe possibly the Tigers . . . If I get down to the St. Louis Browns, then I'll definitely be a writer.

Neil Simon, from
Brighton Beach Memoirs

Leslie Kuter
Autobiographical Art History:
Eakins Concert Singer,
Queen Hatshepsut, and
Josh Gibson, 1978
Wool on burlap

John Dobbs
Follow Thru, c. 1978
Watercolor on paper

The pitcher winding
like a clock—the batter tense
and waiting; the ball and baserunner both heading towards
home; and the crowd, rising as
one when the ball's hit deep.

Ron Cohen
Willie Mays, 1978
Acrylic and oil on canvas

To be a pitcher! I thought. A
pitcher, standing at the axis of event,
or a catcher with the God-view of
the play all before him; to be a
shortstop, lord of the infield, or a
center fielder with unchallenged
claim to all the territory one's speed
and skill could command; to per-
form the spontaneous acrobatics of
the third baseman or the practiced
ballet of the man at second, or to
run and throw with the absolute
commitment of the outfielder! And
to live in a world without grays,
where all decisions were final: ball
or strike, safe or out, the game won
or lost beyond question or appeal.

Eric Rolfe Greenberg, *from*
The Celebrant

Anonymous
Brooklyn Baltics vs. Liberty Nine of New Brunswick, 1870-72
Watercolor on cloth

His art is eccentricity, his aim
How not to hit the mark he seems to aim at,

His passion how to avoid the obvious,
His technique how to vary the avoidance.

The others throw to be comprehended. He
Throws to be a moment misunderstood.

Yet not too much. Not errant, arrant, wild,
But every seeming aberration willed.

Not to, yet still, still to communicate
Making the batter understand too late.

Robert Francis,
"Pitcher"

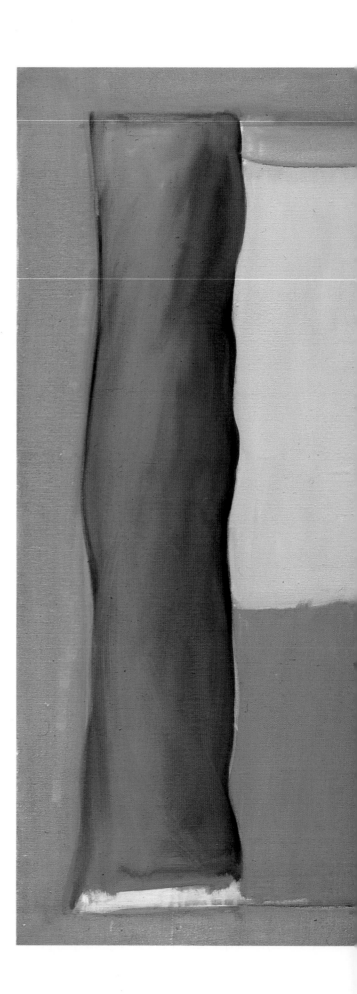

Basil King
Pastorale, 1983
Oil on canvas

John Marin
Baseball, 1953
Colored pencil on paper

Forty years ago and 400 miles from Boston, I sat in my father's Chevrolet, in the Shillington (Pa.) High School parking lot, and listened to the seventh game of the 1946 World Series, the Red Sox vs. the Cardinals. Eighth inning score 3-3, Cardinals up, Enos Slaughter on first base, Harry Walker at the plate; there's a hit to center field, Leon Culberson (substituting for the injured Dom DiMaggio) throws to the infield, shortstop Johnny Pesky cuts it off—Slaughter scores!! The Cardinals hold on to win the game and the World Series. I don't know if I cried, sitting alone in that old Chevrolet, but I was only 14 and well might have. Dazed and with something lost forever, I emerged into the golden September afternoon, where my classmates were jostling and yelling, nuzzling their steadies, sneaking smokes and shooting baskets in a blissful animal innocence I could no longer share.

John Updike, *from*
"Rapt by the Radio"

Elaine de Kooning
Campy at the Plate, 1953-80
Acrylic on canvas

Nelson Rosenberg
Out at Third, no date
Watercolor and gouache

Although I can't remember who won last year's Super
Bowl, I can still remember where I was when Don
Larsen pitched the perfect game, when Bill Mazeroski
hit the "shot heard 'round the world," or when Herb
Score was hit in the eye by Gil McDougald's batted ball.
In those three examples mentioned, I was (1) on an
extended school recess in order to listen in, (2) missing
class by watching the game in the school library, and (3)
listening by transistor radio in the back of the class via
an earphone taped to my wrist . . .

The world is roaring by on its serious, involved
course, but here are some people who have suspended
time and are just enjoying themselves. And to think that
in the major leagues alone, there are over two thousand
of these mini-Woodstocks taking place across the country from spring until fall.

Bob Chieger, from
Voices of Baseball

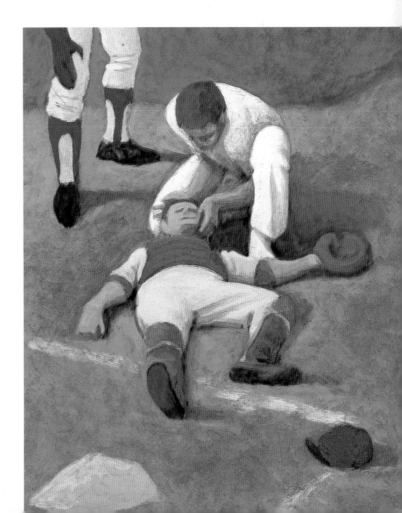

Leonard Dufresne
Injured Catcher, 1975
Acrylic on masonite

Lance Richbourg
Untitled, 1978
Oil on canvas

Game Six, Game Six . . . what can we say of it without seeming to diminish it by recapitulation or dull it with detail? Those of us who were there will remember it, surely, as long as we have any baseball memory, and those who wanted to be there and were not will be sorry always. Crispin Crispian: for Red Sox fans, this was Agincourt. The game also went out to sixty-two million television viewers, a good many millions of whom missed their bedtime. Three days of heavy rains had postponed things; the outfield grass was a lush, Amazon green, but there was a clear sky at last and a welcoming moon—a giant autumn squash that rose above the right-field Fenway bleachers during batting practice.

In silhouette, the game suggests a well-packed but dangerously overloaded canoe —with the high bulge of the Red Sox' three first-inning runs in the bow, then the much bulkier hump of six Cincinnati runs amidships, then the counterbalancing three Boston runs astern, and then, *way* aft, one more shape. But this picture needs colors: Fred Lynn clapping his hands once, quickly and happily, as his three-run opening shot flies over the Boston bullpen and into the bleachers . . . Luis Tiant fanning Perez with a curve and the Low-Flying Plane, then dispatching Foster with a Fall Off the Fence. Luis does not have his fastball, however. . . .

Pete Rose singles in the third. Perez singles in the fourth—his first real contact off Tiant in three games. Rose, up again in the fifth, with a man on base, fights off Tiant for seven pitches, then singles hard to center. Ken Griffey triples off the wall, exactly at the seam of the left-field and center-field angles; Fred Lynn, leaping up for the ball and missing it, falls backward into the wall and comes down heavily. He lies there, inert, in a terrible, awkwardly twisted position, and for an instant all of us think that he has been killed. He is up at last, though, and even stays in the lineup, but the noise and joy are gone out of the crowd, and the game is turned around. Tiant, tired and old and, in the end, bereft even of mannerisms, is rocked again and again—eight hits in three innings—and Johnson removes him, far too late, after Geronimo's first-pitch home run in the eighth has run the score to 6-3 for the visitors.

By now, I had begun to think sadly of distant friends of mine —faithful lifelong Red Sox fans all over New England, all over the East, whom I could almost see sitting silently at home and slowly shaking their heads as winter began to fall on them out of their sets. I scarcely noticed when Lynn led off the eighth with a single and Petrocelli walked. Sparky Anderson, flicking levers like a master back-hoe operator, now

called in Eastwick, his sixth pitcher of the night, who fanned Evans and retired Burleson on a fly. Bernie Carbo, pinch-hitting, looked wholly overmatched against Eastwick, flailing at one inside fastball like someone fighting off a wasp with a croquet mallet. One more fastball arrived, high and over the middle of the plate, and Carbo smashed it in a gigantic, flattened parabola into the center-field bleachers, tying the game. Everyone over there—and everyone in the stands too, I suppose—leaped to his feet and waved both arms exultantly, and the bleachers looked like the dark surface of a lake lashed with a sudden night squall.

The Sox, it will be recalled, nearly won it right away, when they loaded the bases in the ninth with none out, but an ill-advised dash home by Denny Doyle after a fly, and a cool, perfect peg to the plate by George Foster, snipped the chance. The balance of the game now swung back, as it so often does when opportunities are wasted. Drago pitched out of a jam in the tenth, but he flicked Pete Rose's uniform with a pitch to start the eleventh. Griffey bunted, and Fisk snatched up the ball and, risking all, fired to second for the force on Rose. Morgan was next, and I had very little hope left. He struck a drive on a quick, deadly rising line—you could still hear the loud *whock!* in the stands as the

Diamonds Are Forever

THE ROUND TRIPPER

Jim Markowich and Paul Kuhrman
*The Round Tripper (from the Tarot
de Cooperstown)*, 1983
Acrylic and colored pencil on canvas

white blur went out over the infield—and for a moment I thought the ball would land ten or fifteen rows back in the right-field bleachers. But it wasn't hit quite that hard—it was traveling too fast, and there was no sail to it—and Dwight Evans, sprinting backward and watching the flight of it over his shoulder, made a last-second half-staggering turn to his left, almost facing away from the plate at the end, and pulled the ball in over his head at the fence. The great catch made for two outs in the end, for Griffey had never

stopped running and was easily doubled off first.

And so the swing of things was won back again. Carlton Fisk, leading off the bottom of the twelfth against Pat Darcy, the eighth Reds pitcher of the night—it was well into morning now, in fact—socked the second pitch up and out, farther and farther into the darkness above the lights, and when it came down at last, re-illuminated, it struck the topmost, innermost edge of the screen inside the yellow left-field foul pole and glanced sharply down and bounced on the grass: a fair ball, fair all the way. I was watching the ball, of course, so I missed what everyone on television saw— Fisk waving wildly, weaving and writhing and gyrating along the first-base line, as he wished the ball fair, *forced* it fair with his entire body. He circled the bases in triumph, in sudden company with several hundred fans, and jumped on home plate with both feet, and John Kiley, the Fenway park organist, played Handel's "Hallelujah Chorus," *fortissimo*, and then followed with other appropriately exuberant classical selections, and for the second time that evening I suddenly remembered all my old absent and distant Sox-afflicted friends (and all the other Red Sox fans, all over New England), and I thought of them—in Brookline, Mass., and Brooklin, Maine; in Beverly Farms and Mashpee and Presque Isle and North Conway and Damariscotta; in

Pomfret, Connecticut, and Pomfret, Vermont; in Wayland and Providence and Revere and Nashua, and in both the Concords and all five Manchesters; and in Raymond, New Hampshire (where Carlton Fisk was *born*), and I saw all of them dancing and shouting and kissing and leaping about like the fans at Fenway—jumping up and down in their bedrooms and kitchens and living rooms, and in bars and trailers, and even in some boats here and there, I suppose, and on back-country roads (a lone driver getting the news over the radio and blowing his horn over and over, and finally pulling up and getting out and leaping up and down on the cold macadam, yelling into the night), and all of them, for once at least, utterly joyful and believing in that joy —alight with it.

It should be added, of course, that very much the same sort of celebration probably took place the following night in the midlands towns and vicinities of the Reds' supporters—in Otterbein and Scioto; in Frankfort, Sardinia, and Summer Shade; in Zanesville and Louisville and Akron and French Lick and Loveland. I am not enough of a social geographer to know if the faith of the Red Sox fan is deeper or hardier than that of a Reds rooter (although I secretly believe that it may be, because of his longer and more bitter disappointments down the years). What I do know is that this belonging and caring

John Kennard
Shea Stadium, New York, 1983
Photograph

is what our games are all about; this is what we come for. It is foolish and childish, on the face of it, to affiliate ourselves with anything so insignificant and patently contrived and commercially exploitative as a professional sports team, and the amused superiority and icy scorn that the non-fan directs at the sports nut (I know this look—I know it by heart) is understandable and almost unanswerable. Almost. What is left out of this calculation, it seems to me, is the business of caring—caring deeply and passionately, really *caring*—which is a capacity or an emotion that has almost gone out of our lives. And so it seems possible that we have come to a time when it no longer matters so much what the caring is about, how frail or foolish is the object of that concern, as long as the feeling itself can be saved. Naïveté—the infantile and ignoble joy that sends a grown man or woman to dancing and shouting with joy in the middle of the night over the haphazardous flight of a distant ball— seems a small price to pay for such a gift.

Roger Angell, *from* Five Seasons

Now it was Liddle, jerking into motion as Wertz poised at the plate, and then the motion smoothed out and the ball came sweeping in to Wertz, a shoulder-high pitch, a fast ball that probably would have been a fast curve, except that Wertz was coming around and hitting it, hitting it about as hard as I have ever seen a ball hit, on a high line to dead center field.

For whatever it is worth, I have seen such hitters as Babe Ruth, Lou Gehrig, Ted Williams, Jimmy Foxx, Ralph Kiner, Hack Wilson, Johnny Mize, and lesser-known but equally long hitters as Wally Berger and Bob Seeds send the batted ball tremendous distances. None, that I recall, ever hit a ball any harder than this one by Wertz in my presence.

And yet I was not immediately perturbed. I have been a Giant fan for years, twenty-eight years to be exact, and I have seen balls hit with violence to extreme center field which were caught easily by Mays, or Thomson before him, or Lockman or Ripple or Hank Leiber or George Kiddo Davis, that most marvelous fly catcher.

I did not—then—feel alarm, though the crack was loud and clear, and the crowd's roar rumbled behind it like growing thunder. It may be that I did not believe the ball would carry as far as it did, hard hit as it was. I have seen hard-hit balls go a hundred feet into an infielder's waiting glove, and all that one remembers is crack, blur, spank. This ball did not alarm me because it was hit to dead center field

—Mays' territory—and not between the fielders, into those dread alleys in left-center and right-center which lead to the bullpens.

And this was not a terribly high drive. It was a long low fly or a high liner, whichever you wish. This ball was hit not nearly so high as the triple Wertz struck earlier in the day, so I may have assumed that it would soon start to break and dip and come down to Mays, not too far from his normal position.

Then I looked at Willie, and alarm raced through me, peril flaring against my heart. To my utter astonishment, the young Giant center fielder—the inimitable Mays, most skilled of outfielders, unique for his ability to scent the length and direction of any drive and then turn and move to the final destination of the ball—Mays was turned full around, head down, running as hard as he could, straight toward the runway between the two bleacher sections.

I knew then that I had underestimated—badly underestimated—the length of Wertz's blow.

I wrenched my eyes from Mays and took another look at the ball, winging its way along, undipping, unbreaking, forty feet higher than Mays' head, rushing along like a locomotive, nearing Mays, and I thought then: it will beat him to the wall.

Through the years I have tried to do what Red Barber has cautioned me and millions of admiring fans to do: take your eye from the ball after it's been hit and look at the outfielder and the runners. This is a terribly difficult thing to learn; for twenty-five years I was unable to do it. Then I started to take stabs at the fielder and the ball, alternately. Now I do it pretty well. Barber's advice pays off a thousand times in appreciation of what is unfolding, of what takes some six or seven seconds—that's all, six or seven seconds—and of what I can see in several takes, like a jerking motion picture, until I have enough pieces to make nearly a whole.

There is no perfect whole, of course, to a play in baseball. If there was, it would require a God to take it all in. For instance, on such a play, I would like to know what Manager Durocher is doing—leaping to the outer lip of the sunken dugout, bent forward, frozen in anxious fear? And Lopez—is he also frozen, hope high but too anxious to let it swarm through him? The coaches—have they started to wave their arms in joy, getting the runners moving, or are they half-waiting, in fear of the impossible catch and the mad scramble that might ensue on the base paths?

The players—what have they done? The fans—are they standing, or half-crouched, yelling (I hear them, but since I do not see them, I do not know who makes that noise, which of them yells and which is silent)? Has activity stopped in the Giant bullpen where Grissom still had been toiling? Was he now turned to watch the

flight of the ball, the churning dash of Mays?

No man can get the entire picture; I did what I could, and it was painful to rip my sight from one scene frozen forever on my mind, to the next, and then to the next.

I had seen the ball hit, its rise; I had seen Mays' first backward sprint; I had again seen the ball and Mays at the same time, Mays still leading. Now I turned to the diamond—how long does it take the eyes to sweep and focus and telegraph to the brain?—and there was the vacant spot on the hill (how often we see what is not there before we see what is there) where Liddle had been and I saw him at the third-base line, between home and third (the wrong place for a pitcher on such a play; he should be behind third to cover a play there, or behind home to back up a play there, but not in between).

I saw Doby, too, hesitating, the only man, I think, on the diamond who now conceded that Mays might catch the ball. Doby is a center fielder and a fine one and very fast himself, so he knows what a center fielder can do. He must have gone nearly halfway to third, now he was coming back to second base a bit. Of course, he may have known that he could jog home if the ball landed over Mays' head, so there was no need to get too far down the line.

Rosen was as near to second as Doby, it seemed. He had come down from first, and for a second—no, not that long, no—

where near that long, for a hundred-thousandth of a second, more likely—I thought Doby and Rosen were Dark and Williams hovering around second, making some foolish double play on this ball that had been hit three hundred and thirty feet past them. Then my mind cleared; they were in Cleveland uniforms, not Giant, they were Doby and Rosen.

And that is all I allowed my eyes on the inner diamond. Back now to Mays—had three seconds elapsed from the first ominous connection of bat and ball?—and I saw Mays do something that he seldom does and that is so often fatal to outfielders. For the briefest piece of time—I cannot shatter and compute fractions of seconds like some atom gun—Mays started to raise his head and turn it to his left, as though he were about to look behind him.

Then he thought better of it, and continued the swift race with the ball that hovered quite close to him now, thirty feet high and coming down (yes, finally coming down) and again—for the second time—I knew Mays would make the catch.

In the Polo Grounds, there are two square-ish green screens, flanking the runway between the two bleacher sections, one to the left-field side of the runway, the other to the right. The screens are intended to provide a solid dark background for the pitched ball as it comes in to the batter. Otherwise he would be trying to pick out the ball from a far-off sea of shirts of many colors, jackets, balloons, and banners.

Wertz's drive, I could see now, was not going to end up in the runway on the fly; it was headed for the screen on the right-field side.

The fly, therefore, was not the longest ball ever hit in the Polo Grounds, not by a comfortable margin. Wally Berger had hit a ball over the left-field roof around the four-hundred foot marker. Joe Adcock had hit a ball into the center-field bleachers. A Giant pitcher, Hal Schumacher, had once hit a ball over the left-field roof, about as far out as Berger's. Nor—if Mays caught it—would it be the longest ball ever caught in the Polo Grounds. In either the 1936 or 1937 World Series—I do not recall which—Joe DiMaggio and Hank Leiber traded gigantic smashes to the foot of the stairs within that runway; each man had caught the other's. When DiMaggio caught Leiber's, in fact, it meant the third out of the game. DiMaggio caught the ball and barely broke step to go up the stairs and out of sight before the crowd was fully aware of what had happened.

So Mays' catch—if he made it—would not necessarily be in the realm of the improbable. Others had done feats that bore some resemblance to this.

Yet Mays' catch—if, indeed, he was to make it—would dwarf all the others for the simple reason that he, too, could have caught Leiber's or DiMaggio's fly, whereas neither could have caught Wertz's. Those balls had been towering drives, hit so high the outfielder could run forever before the ball came down. Wertz had hit his ball harder and on a lower trajectory. Leiber—not a fast man—was nearing second base when DiMaggio caught his ball; Wertz—also not fast—was at first when . . .

When Mays simply slowed down to avoid running into the wall, put his hands up in cup-like fashion over his left shoulder, and caught the ball much like a football player catching leading passes in the end zone.

He had turned so quickly, and run so fast and truly that he made this impossible catch look—to us in the bleachers—quite ordinary. To those reporters in the press box, nearly six hundred feet from the bleacher wall, it must have appeared far more astonishing, watching Mays run and run until he had become the size of a pigmy and then he had run some more, while the ball diminished to a mote of white dust and finally disappeared in the dark blob that was Mays' mitt.

Arnold Hano, *from*
A Day in the Bleachers

Mauro Altamura
Untitled, 1984
Photograph

That day we played Detroit, and in that game I prayed my first prayer. Clarkson was pitching, Kelly catching. John could sail them over so fast the thermometer would drop two degrees as the ball whizzed past the batter. We had them beat last half ninth, two were on bases, two out, Charley Bennett at bat. Charley could not touch a high-and-in ball, but could kill a low one. John shot one over and it went low—Charley caught it on the nose and out to right center she came. It was up to me. I turned and ran with all my might, and I said: "O God! If ever you helped mortal man in your life, help me get that ball, and you haven't much time to decide." I looked over my shoulder and saw the ball near—I shot out my left hand, the ball struck and stuck. You can't convince me God did not help me that day . . .

Rev. W. A. (Billy) Sunday, from
Collier's

…Time is of the essence. The rhythms break,
 More varied and subtle than any kind of dance;
 Movement speeds up or lags. The ball goes out
 In sharp and angular drives, or long, slow ones,
 Comes in again controlled and under aim;
 The players wheel or sprint, race, stoop, slide,
  halt,
 Shift imperceptibly to new positions,
 Watching the signs, according to the batter,
 The score, the inning. Time is of the essence…

Rolfe Humphries, from
"Polo Grounds"

Howardena Pindell

Baseball Series: Video Drawing (Detail), 1974-76
Color photograph

There was something
about Reddie Ray that
pleased all the senses. His
little form seemed instinct
with life; any sudden movement was suggestive of
stored lightning. His position at the plate was on the
left side, and he stood perfectly motionless, with just
a hint of tense waiting
alertness.

Zane Grey, from
The Redheaded Outfield

James Daugherty
Three Base Hit, 1914
Gouache and ink on paper

Yet the Whammer felt oddly relieved. He liked to have his back crowding the wall, when there was a single pitch to worry about and a single pitch to hit. Then the sweat began to leak out of his pores as he stared at the hard, lanky figure of the pitiless pitcher, moving, despite his years and a few waste motions, like a veteran undertaker of the diamond, and he experienced a moment of depression.

Sam must have sensed it, because he discovered an unexpected pity in his heart and even for a split second hoped the idol would not be tumbled. But only for a second, for the Whammer had regained confidence in his known talent and experience and was taunting the greenhorn to throw.

Someone in the crowd hooted and the Whammer raised aloft two fat fingers and pointed where he would murder the ball, where the gleaming rails converged on the horizon and beyond was invisible.

Roy raised his leg. He smelled the Whammer's blood and wanted it, and through him the worm's he had with him, for the way he had insulted Sam.

The third ball slithered at the batter like a meteor, the flame swallowing itself. He lifted his club to crush it into a universe of sparks but the heavy wood dragged, and though he willed to destroy the sound he heard a gong bong and realized with sadness that the ball he had expected to hit had long since been part of the past; and though Max could not cough the fatal word out of his throat, the Whammer understood he was, in the truest sense of it, out.

The crowd was silent as the violet evening fell on their shoulders.

Bernard Malamud, *from*
The Natural

Jacob Lawrence
Strike, 1949
Tempera on masonite

Mark Rucker

Angel Hermosa's Double Play, 1974

Graphite on paper

In his sea lit
distance, the pitcher winding
like a clock about to chime comes down with

the ball, hit
sharply, under the artificial
banks of arc-lights, bounds like a vanishing string

over the green
to the shortstop magically
scoop to his right whirling above his invisible

shadows
in the dust redirects
its flight to the running poised second baseman

pirouettes
leaping, above the slide, to throw
from mid-air, across the colored tightened interval,

to the leaning-
out first baseman ends the dance
drawing it disappearing into his long brown glove

stretches. What
is too swift for deception
is final, lost, among the loosened figures

jogging off the field
(the pitcher walks), casual
in the space where the poem has happened.

Robert Wallace,
"The Double Play"

John Dobbs
Stretching at First, c. 1976
Oil on canvas

Poised between going on and back, pulled
Both ways taut like a tightrope-walker,
Fingertips pointing the opposites,
Now bouncing tiptoe like a dropped ball
Or a kid skipping rope, come on, come on,
Running a scattering of steps sidewise,
How he teeters, skitters, tingles, teases,
Taunts them, hovers like an ecstatic bird,
He's only flirting, crowd him, crowd him,
Delicate, delicate, delicate, delicate—now!

Robert Francis,
"The Base Stealer"

Susan Grayson
Rickey Henley
    Henderson, 1985
Photographs (16 images)

Leonard Dufresne

Man on Second, 1975

Acrylic on masonite

Kim MacConnell
Green Sliding, 1980
Two-color silkscreen on diecut and folded paper

Somebody is always trying to improve baseball. A few years ago, a fan sent me an ingenious proposal designed to add variety and zest to the old game by means of one small shift in the rules: a batter who had just struck the ball or who had drawn ball four would have the option of heading for first base *or third base*. If he selected the latter route, he would then be required to proceed around the bases in the same startling clockwise direction, and his ensuing fortunes and adventures along the way would be governed by the existing rules of the game. I regret that I have forgotten the author of this inspired document (it was subsequently published and reprinted in several sporting journals), for his little swerve or jiggle in the straitlaced laws of the pastime offers more possibilities for surprise and entertainment than one might at first suppose. The scheme and its results are still sometimes talked about in dugouts and bullpens around the leagues. Think about it. Let's say that our batsman steps up to the plate with no outs and teammate on first base, and taps a routine bouncer toward first—a good chance for a double play, you say, except that the batter, exercising his new option, sensibly sprints north instead of south, while the runner at first, now no longer subject to the force play, holds his base. The first baseman, fielding the ball, halts in mid-pivot when he notices that there will be no play at second, then realizes that there will be nothing doing at first base either, and at last gets off his peg to third, far too late for the out. Base hit, runners at first and third; still no outs. As it happens, both these baserunners are quick and each now takes a good lead off his base. The pitcher anxiously throws over to first a couple of times, to keep the runner close, then tries a pickoff at third. No luck. He delivers a strike, then a ball, and on the next pitch both runners take off for second. The pitch is low and away to the right-handed batter, slightly discomposing the catcher; his good peg is a hair late, and both sliding runners are safe out there (a double palms-down gesture by the ump), where they greet each other with double handslaps and help dust off each other's pants.

Other possibilities now suggest themselves. If the game were a close one (or even if it *weren't* close, now that I think about it) both men would

Harvey Breverman
Beckett and Baseball, 1986
Pastel on paper

immediately try to steal the next base, given the absolute guarantee that at least one of them would be safe and now in scoring position. If both were safe, and if the flustered pitcher understandably lost his control for a bit, we might soon find *two* baserunners at each corner. Now what? Now a sacrifice fly to medium-deep center field, please, with the two inbound runners tagging up after the catch and both—arriving at opposite corners of the plate in converging clouds of dust—just beating the throw home ("Ah, there, José" . . . Can it be you again, *amigo* Dwayne?"), while both outbound men trot along to second on the play. In no time, one can envisage, the bases might be loaded—and I mean *loaded*—and the next man. . . . No, it won't work. The possibilities have begun to outweigh our anticipations, the umpires are overburdened, and pity for the pitcher and the infield defense dims our wish for further wonders—a double rundown between second and third, say, or a six-run triple to deep center, with the concentric circles of baserunners whirling about the basepaths in a double pinwheel of overpopulation and, yes, ennui. Baseball, we understand once again, is spare and rigorous by nature, and is also somehow *right*. We can ignore it or hate it, if that is our choice, but we must take it as it is. It cannot be better.

Roger Angell, *from*
Baseball

Scott Mlyn
Yankee and Fans, Yankee
Stadium, New York, 1980
Photograph

All baseball fans can be divided into two groups: those who come to batting practice and the others. Only those in the first category have much chance of amounting to anything . . .

The fan's leisurely arrival while the ball park is nearly empty, the slowly-paced first hot-dog-and-beer, the meticulous filling out of the scorecard, the calm perusal of the visitors taking their licks . . . all this is part of adapting the spirit to baseball's deliberate speed and its demand for heightened awareness of detail. Especially at evening, when the sky itself darkens like the stage lights dimming, there is a coexistence of total relaxation and keen anticipation that is totally lost on the fan who rushes to his seat to beat the first pitch.

Thomas Boswell, from
How Life Imitates the World Series

The crowd at the ball game
is moved uniformly

by a spirit of uselessness
which delights them—

all the exciting detail
of the chase

and the escape, the error
the flash of genius—

all to no end save beauty
the eternal—

So in detail they, the crowd,
are beautiful

for this
to be warned against

saluted and defied—
It is alive, venomous

it smiles grimly
its words cut—

The flashy female with her
mother, gets it—

The Jew gets it straight—it
is deadly, terrifying—

It is the inquisition, the
Revolution

It is beauty itself
that lives

day by day in them
idly—

This is
the power of their faces

It is summer, it is the solstice
the crowd is

cheering, the crowd is laughing
in detail

permanently, seriously
without thought

William Carlos Williams,
"At the Ball Game"

Arnold Friedman
World Series, c. 1930-38
Oil on canvas

The true zealot wants his baseball with him everywhere he goes, even to bed, where he can play it electronically on the ceiling, or by inventing his own private league (as in Robert Coover's classic book "Universal Baseball Association Inc., J. Henry Waugh, Prop.") or by phoning a fellow addict for relief. But for the average citizen, simply trotting out onto the spring grass, and maybe backhanding a grounder and flipping it, and bathing one's ears once more in the immemorial chatter—"Only takes one to hit one," "'S'lookin' em over," "No pitcher, no pitcher"—will do.

To such a fan, an American summer without those sounds would be as empty as Rachel Carson's "Silent Spring." Those piping chirps of "A walk's as good as a hit" are like crickets in August. Where do they go in the winter, anyway? Some fly South, others disappear into the closet, where, I suspect, fans mouth them silently as they pound their mitts.

But right now the voice of the umpire is heard once again in the land, the ducks are on the pond and the goose hangs high. The season isn't over till it's over, but the clichés can already beat you a lot of ways. If the mark of a grand passion is that you can love it even when it's kind of dumb, then baseball wins out by inches, one game at a time. Baseball is pre-eminently the talking man's game and who cares, or even notices, if the conversation is sometimes awesomely dull?

Wilfrid Sheed, *from*
"Diamonds Are Forever,"
The New York Times Magazine

Robert Gwathmey
World Series #2, 1958
Watercolor and pencil on paper

The one damn time (7th inning)
standing up to get a hot dog someone spills
mustard all over me.

> **The conception is**
the hit, whacko!
Likewise out of the park

of our own indifferent vulgarity, not
mind you, that one repents even the most visual
satisfaction.

Early in life the line is straight
made straight
against the grain.

Take the case of myself, and why not
since these particulars need
no further impetus

> **take me at the age of 13**
and for some reason there, no matter the particular
reason.

> **The one damn time (7th inning)**
standing up to get a hot dog someone spills
mustard all over me.

Robert Creeley,
"The Ball Game"

"Let him stay up there!" the man from Jersey City shouted. "Let him win his own game." He turned to his public. "I would like to see old Ben smack one out and win the ball game," he said, "and go right over to Terry and spit in his face."

But old Ben didn't get a chance. Grimes put a man called Spence in to bat for him and Spence popped out.

In the next inning the Brooklyn second baseman juggled a ball and another run scored. All hope fled from the dark Greek face. "Why is it," he asked, "that other teams don't do it?" He got up, preparing to leave. "A man on third and one out," he said, "and no score. They ought to shoot Grimes for that. No jury would convict. Ah," he said, moving down toward the exit gate, "I'm going to root for a winning team from now on. I've been rooting for a losing team long enough. I'm going to root for the Giants. You don't know," he said to the Brooklyn fan moving along with him, "you don't know the pleasure you get out of rooting for a winning team."

And he went back to Jersey City, leaving his heart in Brooklyn.

Irwin Shaw, from
"No Jury Would Convict"

Tod Papageorge

Shea Stadium, 1970

Gelatin-silver print

When Harry Ruby, the songwriter, died in California, the obituary bestowed the title of "world's greatest baseball fan" on the composer of "Three Little Words," "Who's Sorry Now?," "Baby Face" and many other hits. The obit didn't tell the half of it. Harry Ruby felt deeply about music, yet given his choice of composing Beethoven's Third or ripping a line drive over second like Bill Dickey, he would have suited up on the spot. He loved the piano but would infinitely rather have been Pete Rose than Artur Rubinstein.

In Hollywood he adjusted his working hours according to the Pacific Coast League schedule so he could be in the Wrigley Field or the old Hollywood Stars park early and work out with the professionals. When big league teams like the Pirates, Cubs, White Sox and Philadelphia Athletics trained in California, Harry was always welcome to shag flies in the outfield. In those days he wore the livery of the Washington Senators, a gift that he prized above any other possession. When the westward movement of the majors brought him into contact with other clubs he acquired other uniforms; before he died he could have fitted out an All-Star team from his own wardrobe.

There came a time—this was a good many years ago—when Harry felt a need for change. Nothing heretical like taking up golf or developing an interest in pro football, but some break in the routine that might broaden his outlook.

Travel, he decided, would do the trick. He would visit places where he had never been, view sights he had never seen, sample food and observe the customs of people in far lands, and come home with a fresh slant that would express itself in his work. He might even be able to provide his lyricist, Bert Kalmar, with a new rhyme for "eyes" or "moon."

After consulting travel agents, he fixed upon a Mediterranean cruise. This was early in the season, and all summer long he went about the studio lots with his pocket seven months gone with travel literature that he would break out and display with or without provocation.

"Did I tell you about my trip? Look, we sail from New York and the first stop is here in Gibraltar. Wait, I got something here tells about the Rock. Then it's Barcelona, Marseilles, and how do you pronounce it? Cannes? From there . . ."

His enthusiasm was infectious at first, but it was a long, hot summer. By the time Harry's friends had been twice through the itinerary they were ducking for cover or beating him to the conversational draw with "Harry, do you think this young Judnich with Oakland will ever play the outfield like Jigger Statz?" or "Hey, I see your friend Lefty O'Doul is leading the league again. Isn't he ever going to give up?"

If they could get Harry talking baseball they could usually escape without being shown another picture of the Acropolis, provided they were fast on their feet.

At long last the Coast League playoffs ended. (San Diego won four straight from Sacramento while Portland was beating San Francisco, then the Padres knocked over the Beavers in four.) Harry got to New York in time to see the Yankees defeat the Giants in the World Series. His ship sailed a few days later. In his luggage were several baseballs and a couple of fielder's gloves, and sneakers in addition to his spikes.

On the second day out, Harry found a deck steward who was a baseball fan. "Wait here," Harry said, and darted for his cabin. He returned wearing flannels and sneakers, carrying a ball and two gloves. That day, and every other day

Helen Levitt
New York, 1972
Dye transfer photograph

during the crossing, he and the steward played catch on the sports deck.

When the ship reached port, Harry and the steward were among the first down the gang-plank. They found an open space on the pier, and, as eager sightseers streamed past, they played catch.

It happened at Barcelona, Marseilles and Cannes. It happened at Naples, Piraeus and Istanbul. It happened at Port Said, Algiers and Casablanca.

Harry got home a rejuvenated man, and a traveled one. He had not seen a cathedral nor a museum. He had not bought a

hookah in the bazaar in Istanbul nor a drink in the Casbah. But his arm was never so loose, his control never better.

Red Smith,
"The World's Greatest Fan"

I love baseball,
you know it doesn't have to mean anything,
it's just very beautiful to watch.

Woody Allen, *from*
Zelig

"Something Else"

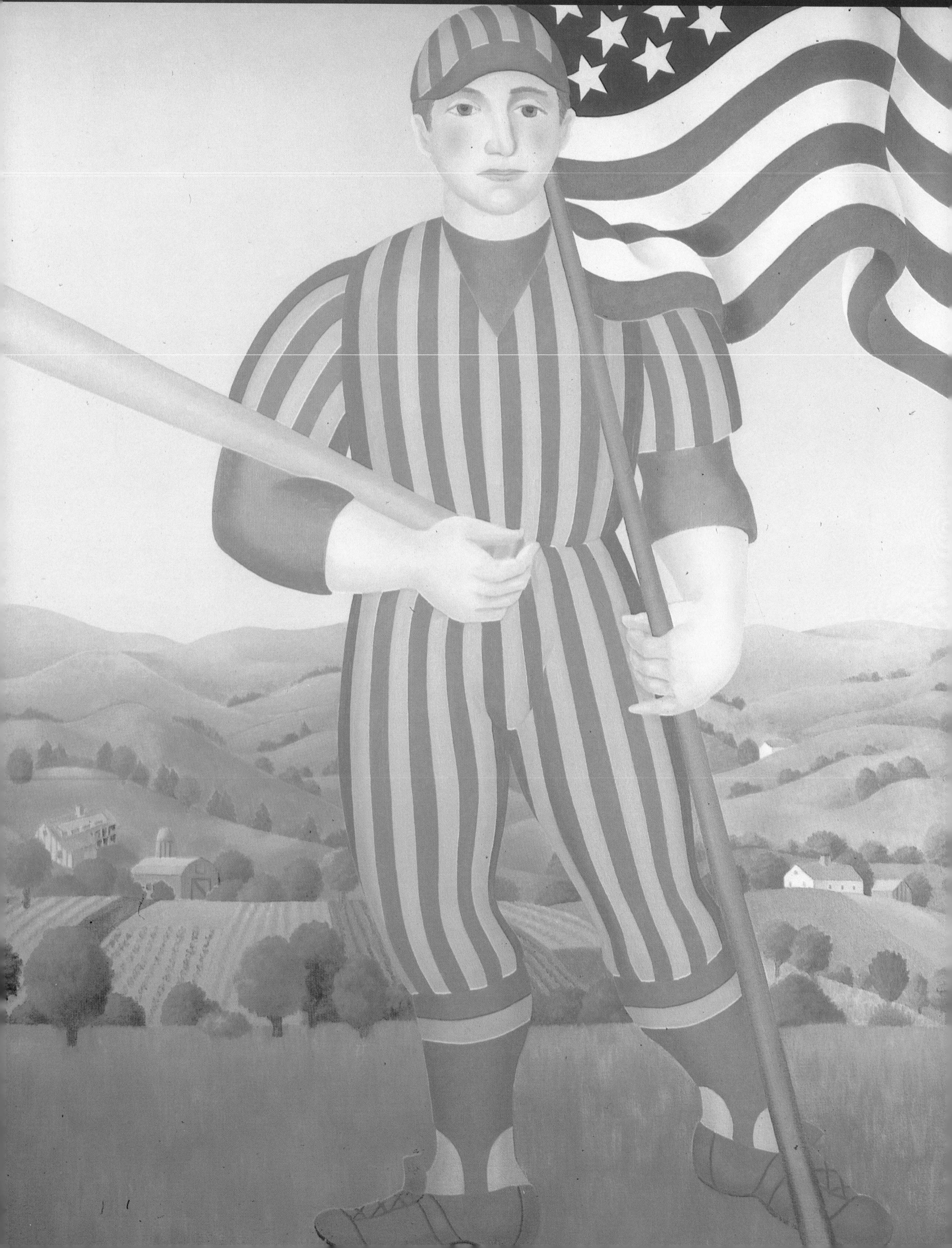

Gregory Thorp
Triple A-143, 1979
Cibachrome photograph

Fathers and sons;
the sounds and smells of
a summer night; listening to
the game on the car radio; and
the cosmic struggles that all games
can come to represent.

Gerald Garston
Pastime, 1984
Oil on canvas

Jed Devine
Untitled, 1985
Palladium print

Whoever wants to know
the heart and mind of America
had better learn baseball . . .

Jacques Barzun, from
"God's Country and Mine"

In one of his essays George Orwell writes that, though he was not very good at the game, he had a long, hopeless love affair with cricket until he was sixteen. My relations with baseball were similar. Between the ages of nine and thirteen, I must have put in a forty-hour week during the snowless months over at the neighborhood playfield—softball, hardball, and stickball pick-up games—while simultaneously holding down a full-time job as a pupil at the local grammar school. As I remember it, news of two of the most cataclysmic public events of my childhood —the death of President Roosevelt and the bombing of Hiroshima—reached me while I was out playing ball. My performance was uniformly erratic; generally okay for those easygoing pick-up games, but invariably lacking the calm and the expertise that the naturals displayed in stiff competition. My taste, and my talent, such as it was, was for the flashy, whiz-bang catch rather than the towering fly; running and leaping I loved, all the do-or-die stuff—somehow I lost confidence waiting and waiting for the ball lofted right at me to descend. I could never make the high school team, yet I remember that, in one of the two years I vainly (in both senses of the word) tried out, I did a good enough imitation of a baseball player's *style* to be able to fool (or amuse) the coach right down to the day he cut the last of the dreamers from the squad and gave out the uniforms.

Though my disappointment was keen, my misfortune did not necessitate a change in plans for the future. Playing baseball was not what the Jewish boys of our lower-middle-class neighborhood were expected to do in later life for a living. Had I been cut from the high school itself, *then* there would have been hell to pay in my house, and much confusion and shame in me. As it was, my family took my chagrin in stride and lost no more faith in me than I actually did in myself. They probably would have been shocked if I had made the team.

Maybe I would have been too. Surely it would have put me on a somewhat different footing with this game that I loved with all my heart, not simply for the fun of playing it (fun was secondary, really), but for the mythic and aesthetic dimension that it gave to an American boy's life—particularly to one whose grandparents could hardly speak English. For someone whose roots in America were strong but only inches deep, and who had no experience, such as a

Catholic child might, of an awesome hierarchy that was real and felt, baseball was a kind of secular church that reached into every class and region of the nation and bound millions upon millions of us together in common concerns, loyalties, rituals, enthusiasms, and antagonisms. Baseball made me understand what patriotism was about, at its best.

Not that Hitler, the Bataan Death March, the battle for the Solomons, and the Normandy invasion didn't make of me and my contemporaries what may well have been the most patriotic generation of schoolchildren in American history

(and the most willingly and successfully propagandized). But the war we entered when I was eight had thrust the country into what seemed to a child —and not only to a child—a struggle to the death between Good and Evil. Fraught with perilous, unthinkable possibilities, it inevitably nourished a patriotism grounded in moral virtue and bloody-minded hate, the patriotism that fixes a bayonet to a Bible. It seems to me that through baseball I was put in touch with a more humane and tender brand of patriotism, lyrical rather than martial or righteous in spirit, and without

Ed Paschke
Mask Man, 1970
Lithograph

the reek of saintly zeal, a patriotism that could not so easily be sloganized, or contained in a high-sounding formula to which you had to pledge something vague but all-encompassing called your "allegiance."

To sing the National Anthem in the school auditorium every week, even during the worst of the war years, generally left me cold. The enthusiastic lady teacher waved her arms in the air and we obliged with the words: "See! Light! Proof! Night! There!" But nothing stirred within, strident as we might be—in the end, just another school exercise. It was different, however, on Sundays out at Ruppert Stadium, a green wedge of pasture miraculously walled in among the factories, warehouses, and truck depots of industrial Newark. It would, in fact, have seemed to me an emotional thrill forsaken if, before the Newark Bears took on the hated enemy from across the marshes, the Jersey City Giants, we hadn't first to rise to our feet (my father, my brother, and I—along with our inimical countrymen, the city's Germans, Italians, Irish, Poles, and, out in the Africa of the bleachers, Newark's Negroes) to celebrate the America that had given to this unharmonious mob a game so grand and beautiful.

Just as I first learned the names of the great institutions of higher learning by trafficking in football pools for a neighborhood bookmaker rather than from our high school's college adviser, so my feel for the American landscape came less from what I learned in the classroom about Lewis and Clark than from following the major-league clubs on their road trips and reading about the minor leagues in the back pages of *The Sporting News*. The size of the continent got through to you finally when you had to stay up to 10:30 p.m. in New Jersey to hear via radio "ticker-tape" Cardinal pitcher Mort Cooper throw the first strike of the night to Brooklyn shortstop Pee Wee Reese out in "steamy" Sportsmen's Park in St. Louis, Missouri. And however much we might be told by teacher about the stockyards and the Haymarket riot, Chicago only began to exist for me as a real place, and to matter in American history, when I became fearful (as a Dodger fan) of the bat of Phil Cavarretta, first baseman for the Chicago Cubs.

Not until I got to college and was introduced to literature did I find anything with a comparable emotional atmosphere and aesthetic appeal. I don't mean to suggest that it was a simple exchange, one passion for another. Between first discovering the Newark Bears and the Brooklyn Dodgers at seven or eight and first looking into Conrad's *Lord Jim* at age eighteen, I had done some growing up. I am only saying that my discovery of literature, and fiction particularly, and the "love affair"—to some degree hopeless, but still earnest—that has ensued, derives in part from this childhood infatuation with baseball. Or, more accurately perhaps, baseball—with its lore and legends, its cultural power, its seasonal associations, its native authenticity, its simple rules and transparent strategies, its longueurs and thrills, its spaciousness, its suspensefulness, its heroics, its nuances, its lingo, its "characters," its peculiarly hypnotic tedium, its mythic transformation of the immediate—was the literature of my boyhood.

Baseball, as played in the big leagues, was something completely outside my own life that could nonetheless move me to ecstasy and to tears; like fiction it could excite the imagination and hold the attention as much with minutiae as with high drama. Mel Ott's cocked leg striding into the ball, Jackie Robinson's pigeon-toed shuffle as he moved out to second base, each was to be as deeply

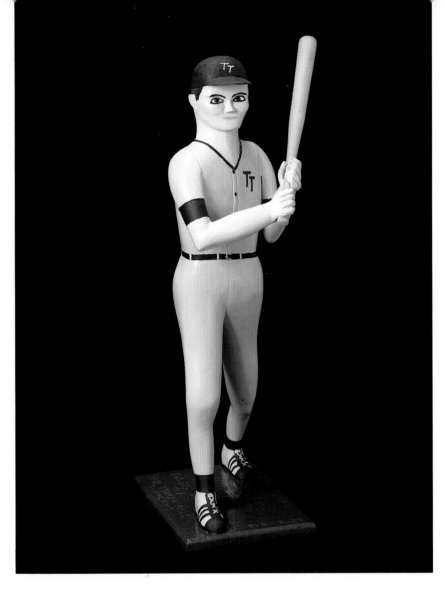

Lavern Kelley
Bass Wood of the
Tinkerville Tomcats, 1987
Enamel paint and wood

a soft country-parson tone to his voice. For the adventures of "dem bums" of Brooklyn—a region then the very symbol of urban wackiness and tumult—to be narrated from Red Barber's highly alien but loving perspective constituted a genuine triumph of what my English professors would later teach me to call "point of view." James himself might have admired the implicit cultural ironies and the splendid possibilities for oblique moral and social commentary. And as for the detail about Rex Barney eating his hot dog, it was irresistible, joining as it did the spectacular to the mundane, and furnishing an adolescent boy with a glimpse of an unexpectedly ordinary, even humdrum, side to male heroism.

Of course, in time, neither the flavor and suggestiveness of Red Barber's narration or "epiphanies" as resonant with meaning as Rex Barney's pregame hot dog could continue to satisfy a developing literary appetite; nonetheless, it was just this that helped to sustain me until I was ready to begin to respond to the great inventors of narrative detail and masters of narrative voice and perspective like James, Conrad, Dostoevsky, and Bellow.

affecting over the years as that night—"inconceivable," "inscrutable," as any night Conrad's Marlow might struggle to comprehend—the night that Dodger wild man, Rex Barney (who never lived up to "our" expectations, who should have been "our" Koufax), not only went the distance without walking in half a dozen runs, but, of all things, threw a no-hitter. A thrilling

mystery, marvelously enriched by the fact that a light rain had fallen during the early evening, and Barney, figuring the game was going to be postponed, had eaten a hot dog just before being told to take the mound.

This detail was passed on to us by Red Barber, the Dodger radio sportscaster of the forties, a respectful, mild Southerner with a subtle rural tanginess to his vocabulary and

Philip Roth,
"My Baseball Years"

It breaks your heart. It is designed to break your heart. The game begins in the spring, when everything else begins again, and it blossoms in the summer, filling the afternoons and evenings, and then as soon as the chill rains come, it stops and leaves you to face the fall alone. You count on it, rely on it to buffer the passage of time, to keep the memory of sunshine and high skies alive, and then just when the days are all twilight, when you need it most, it stops. Today, October 2, a Sunday of rain and broken branches and leaf-clogged drains and slick streets, it stopped, and summer was gone.

Somehow, the summer seemed to slip by faster this time. Maybe it wasn't this summer, but all the summers that, in this my fortieth summer, slipped by so fast. There comes a time when every summer will have something of autumn about it. Whatever the reason, it seemed to me that I was investing more and more in baseball, making the game do more of the work that keeps time fat and slow and lazy. I was counting on the game's deep patterns, three strikes, three outs, three times three innings, and its deepest impulse, to go out and back, to leave and to return home, to set the order of the day and to organize the daylight. I wrote a few things this last summer, this summer that did not last, nothing grand but some things, and yet that work was just camouflage. The real activity was done with the radio—not the all-seeing, all-falsifying television—and was the playing of the game in the only place it will last, the enclosed, green field of the mind. There, in that warm, bright place, what the old poet called Mutability does not so quickly come.

A. Bartlett Giamatti, from
"The Green Fields of the Mind"

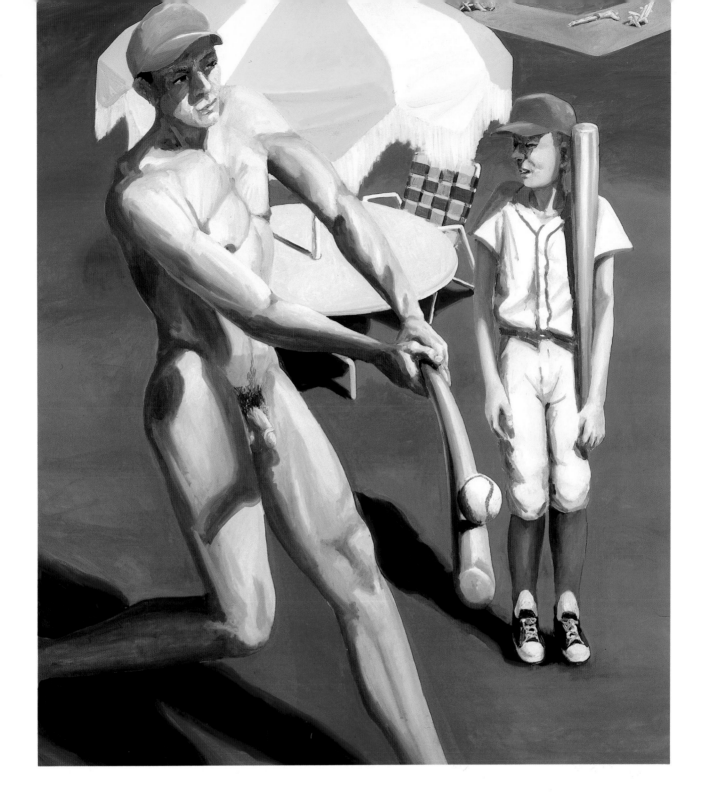

Eric Fischl
Boys at Bat, 1979
Oil on canvas

   Baseball is fathers and sons. Football is brothers beating each other up in the backyard, violent and superficial. Baseball is the generations, looping backward forever with a million apparitions of sticks and balls, cricket and rounders, and the games the Iroquois played in Connecticut before the English came. Baseball is fathers and sons playing catch, lazy and murderous, wild and controlled, the profound archaic song of birth, growth, age, and death. This diamond encloses what we are.

Donald Hall, *from*
"Fathers Playing Catch with Sons"

The game of baseball has always been linked in my mind with the mystic texture of childhood, with the sounds and smells of summer nights and with the memories of my father.

My love for baseball was born on the first day my father took me to Ebbets Field in Brooklyn. Riding in the trolley car, he seemed as excited as I was, and he never stopped talking; now describing for me the street in Brooklyn where he had grown up, now recalling the first game he had been taken to by his own father, now recapturing for me his favorite memories from the Dodgers of his youth—the Dodgers of Casey Stengel, Zach Wheat, and Jimmy Johnston.

In the evenings, when my dad came home from work, we would sit together on our porch and relive the events of that afternoon's game which I had so carefully preserved in the large, red scorebook I'd been given for my seventh birthday. I can still remember how proud I was to have mastered all those strange and wonderful symbols that permitted me to recapture, in miniature form, the every movement of Jackie Robinson and Pee Wee Reese, Duke Snider and Gil Hodges. But the real power of that scorebook lay in the responsibility it entailed. For all through my childhood, my father kept from me the knowledge that the daily papers printed daily box scores, allowing me to believe that without my personal renderings of all those games he missed while he was at work, he would be unable to follow our team in the only proper way a team should be followed, day by day, inning by inning. In other words, without me, his love for baseball would be forever incomplete.

To be sure, there were risks involved in making a commitment as boundless as mine. For me, as for all too many Brooklyn fans, the presiding memory of "the boys of summer" was the memory of the final playoff game in 1951 against the Giants. Going into the ninth, the Dodgers held a 4-1 lead. Then came two singles and a double, placing the winning run at the plate with Bobby Thomson at bat. As Dressen replaced Erskine with Branca, my older sister, with maddening foresight, predicted the forever famous Thomson homer—a prediction that left me so angry with her, imagining that with her words she had somehow brought it about, that I would not speak to her for days.

So the seasons of my childhood passed until that miserable summer when the Dodgers were taken away to Los Angeles by the unforgivable O'Malley, leaving all our rash hopes and dreams of glory behind. And then came a summer of still deeper sadness when my father died. Suddenly my feelings for baseball seemed an aspect of my departing youth, along with my childhood freckles and my favorite childhood haunts, to be left behind when I went away to college and never came back.

Then one September day, having settled into teaching at Harvard, I agreed, half reluctantly, to go to Fenway Park. There it was again: the cozy ballfield scaled to human dimensions so that every word of encouragement and every scornful yell could be heard on the field; the fervent crowd that could, with equal passion, curse a player for today's failures after cheering his heroics the day before; the team that always seemed to break your heart in the last week of the season. It took only a matter of minutes before I found myself directing all my old intensities toward my new team —the Boston Red Sox.

I am often teased by my women friends about my obsession, but just as often, in the most unexpected places— in academic conferences, in literary discussions, at the most elegant dinner parties—I find other women just as crazily committed to baseball as I am, and the discovery creates an instant bond between us. All at once, we are deep in conversation, mingling together the past and the present, as if the history of the Red Sox had been our history too.

There we stand, one moment recollecting the unparalleled performance of Yaz in '67, the next sharing ideas on how the present lineup should be changed; one moment recapturing the splendid career of "the Splendid Splinter," the next complaining about the manager's decision to pull the pitcher the night before. And then, invariably, comes the most vivid memory of all, the frozen image of Carlton Fisk as he rounded first in the sixth game of the '75 World Series, an image as intense in its evocation of triumph as the image of Ralph Branca weeping in the dugout is in its portrayal of heartache.

There is another, more personal memory associated with Carlton Fisk, for he was, after all the years I had followed baseball, the first player I actually met in person. Apparently, he had read the biography I had written on Lyndon Johnson and wanted to meet me. Yet when the meeting took place, I found myself reduced to the shyness of childhood. There I was, a professor at Harvard, accustomed to speaking with presidents of the United States, and yet, standing beside this young man in a baseball uniform, I was speechless.

Finally, Fisk said that it must have been an awesome experience to work with a man of such immense power as President Johnson—and with that, I was at last able to stammer out, with a laugh, "Not as awesome as the thought that I am really standing here talking with you."

Perhaps I have circled back to my childhood, but if this is

so, I am certain that my journey through time is connected in some fundamental way to the fact that I am now a parent myself, anxious to share with my three sons the same ritual I once shared with my father.

For in this linkage between the generations rests the magic of baseball, a game that has defied the ravages of modern life, a game that is still played today by the same basic rules and at the same pace as it was played 100 years ago. There is something deeply satisfying in the knowledge of this continuity.

And there is something else as well which I have experienced sitting in Fenway Park with my small boys on a warm summer's day. If I close my

eyes against the sun, all at once I am back at Ebbets Field, a young girl once more in the presence of my father, watching the players of my youth on the grassy field below. There is magic in this moment, for when I open my eyes and see my sons in the place where my father once sat, I feel an invisible bond between our three generations, an anchor of loyalty linking my sons to the grandfather whose face they never saw but whose person they have already come to know through this most timeless of all sports, the game of baseball.

Doris Kearns Goodwin,
"From Father, with Love"

Nicholas Nixon
Adams Street,
    Watertown, MA, 1977
Photograph

The captains began to take more time in their picking. They considered and consulted and looked down the line before calling out a name. The Badger pounded quick, steady socks in the pocket of his glove while beside him Purdy slowly flapped the jaws of his first baseman's mitt. Soon there were more that had been chosen than that hadn't. The ones who were picked frisked and giggled behind their captains while the ones who hadn't were statues on display. "You," the captains said now, still weighing abilities but unenthusiastic. Finally they just pointed. The Badger walked along the straggling line of leftovers like a general reviewing troops, stood in front of his next man and jerked his thumb back over his shoulder. When there was only one spot left for even teams Denzel and the thin boy were left standing. It was Badger's pick.

Denzel stood at ease, eyes blank. It grew quiet. He felt the others checking him over and he smelled something. Topps bubble gum, the kind that came with baseball cards. He snuck a glance at the thin boy. His eyes were wide, fixed on the Badger, pleading. He had a round little puff of a catcher's mitt that looked like a red pincushion. There was no sign of a baseball ever having landed on it, no dent of a pocket.

Denzel felt the Badger considering him for a moment, eyes dipping to the thick-fingered old-timer's glove, but then he turned and gave a slight, exasperated nod to the thin boy. "We got him."

John Sayles, *from*
The Pride of the Bimbos

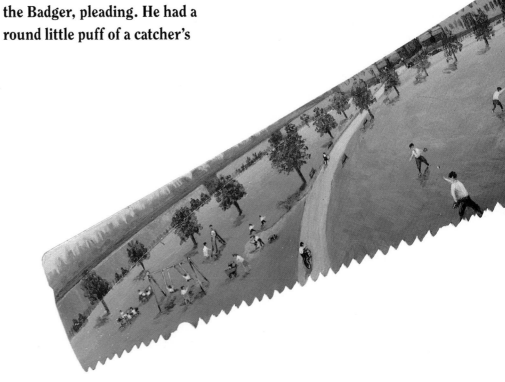

Jacob Kass
Picking a Team, 1985
Oil on saw blade

"Picking a team"

Baseball connects American males with each other, not only through bleacher friendships and neighbor loyalties, not only through barroom fights but, most importantly, through generations. When you are small, you may not discuss politics or union dues or profit margins with your father's cigar-smoking friends when your father has gone out for a six-pack, but you may discuss baseball. It is all you have in common because your father's friend does not wish to discuss the assistant principal or Alice Bisbee Morgan. About the season's moment you know as much as he does; both of you may shake your heads over Lefty's wildness or the rookie who was called out last Saturday when he tried to steal home with two out in the ninth inning and his team down by one.

And you learn your first lessons of the rainbow arc all living makes but that baseball exaggerates. For when you are in sixth grade, the rook has fuzz on his face and throws to the wrong base; before you leave junior high school, he is a seasoned regular, his body filled out, his jowl rippled with tobacco; when you graduate from high school, he is a grizzled veteran —even if you are not certain what *grizzled* means. In a few years the green shoot becomes the withered stalk, and you learn the shape of the hill all beings travel down.

Donald Hall, *from*
"Baseball and the Meaning of Life"

In baseball, you see,
no one ever believes
he's really lost it.

Thomas Boswell, *from*
How Life Imitates the World Series

Walter Iooss, Jr.
Three-Quarter Century
* League Softball, St.*
* Petersburg, Florida*, 1973
Photograph

well, what is this game? i'd like to think it is peculiarly "american," but i can't see any reason to do that aside from the empirical one that it grew up here and has few relatives anywhere else. it's a game in which time and space are warped into totally artificial limits, and i suppose that's part of it: games, after all, have always seemed to me to involve the suspension of reality so we can mess with a specific number of variables inside a rigid framework, thus getting away, for a little bit, from the hassle called life. well, by golly, it sure happens—sometimes so much that nothing happens. the dream is of a game that goes on and on, the last out never being made—or a batter fouling, fouling, fouling, so that no ball is ever fair and again the game goes on. thus time and space so carefully denoted are forever destroyed, or at least put on the shelf. i'm talking about that sag of spirit when you realize in the top of the ninth that you're five runs ahead and that unless the other team scores five the game will be over and you won't get to bat again. it happens to me whether i am playing or watching. *i want the game to go on*. that's an unrealistic view of the universe.

joel oppenheimer, *from*
The Wrong Season

For James Tate

This morning I argued with a friend
about angels. I didn't believe
in his belief in them—I can't
believe they're not a metaphor.
Our argument, affectionate,
lacking in animus, went nowhere.
We promised to talk again soon.
Now, when I'm driving away
from Boston and the Red Sox
are losing, I hear the announcer
say, "No angels in the sky today"—
baseball-ese for *a cloudless afternoon*,
no shadows to help a man
who waits in the outfield
staring into the August sun.
Although I know the announcer's
not a rabbi or sage (no,
he's a sort of sage, disconsolate
philosopher of batting slumps
and injuries), still I scan
the pale blue sky through my
polarized windshield, fervently
hopeful for my fading team
and I feel something a little
foolish, a prayerful throbbing
in my throat and remember
being told years ago that men
are only little lower than
the angels. Floating ahead of me
at the Vermont border, I see
a few wispy horsemane clouds
which I quietly pray will drift
down to Fenway Park where
a demonic opponent has just
slammed another Red Sox pitch,
and the center fielder—call him Jim—
runs back, back, back,
looking heavenward,
and is shielded and doesn't lose
the white ball in the glare.

Sidney Tillim
A Dream of Being, 1968-69
Oil on canvas

Gail Mazur,
"Listening to Baseball in the Car"

My brother would let no one but me
carry his glove or hand him his bat.
I swing a straight stick, he'd say.
Which meant far, far more
than the frozen rope drives
and balls that would rise
high as if never to come down.
Swinging a straight stick talked
—Watch my step. It goes
to all the right places.—
And there were none but the envious
who wouldn't turn to watch him
when his time came to bat.
And even then would pause to weigh
the sound of his wood and wonder
how so much could come unstuck
with just the swing of his stick.
I would have hugged that glove

if I hadn't known to hold it loose
with as much care as I could.
I'd lay his bat by the others . . .
certainly with a measured separation
—set it so no player would dare
mistakenly take it to the plate.
But then came that muggy summer day
when he let Kosko's sister
carry that bat; glove at breasts.
I died that night.
It was a long grayness of running
stumbling awkward . . . never knowing
reaching the home plate of my sleep.
And the next day, my eyes alone
watching from a bleacher seat in back
watching him swing his straight stick
as Kosko's sister snickered and slid
her shorts softly rocking on wooden seat.
I knew from the quick jests and jeers
that others knew. And Kosko, too.
Because he stood on that mound
body bent slightly in . . . ball tight
in grasp that showed knuckles white.
He moved with no nervousness
no casual glancing in stiff fear.
And there my brother dug in deep
cockily at the plate . . . swinging slow.
Kosko pulled his arm back
poised on one leg too thick
and threw that ball so hard
it bounced back arched to himself.
And he caught it easily on the fly
just as my brother, fell, head split
on his stick no longer straight.

Paul Weinman,
"He Swings a Straight Stick"

Steve Gianakos
Untitled, 1981
Acrylic on canvas

Elbert Davis
Death of an Umpire, no date
Oil on linen

Against the bright
grass the white-knickered
players tense, seize,
and attend. A moment
ago, outfielders
and infielders adjusted
their clothing, glanced
at the sun and settled
forward, hands on knees;
the pitcher walked back

of the hill, established
his cap and returned;
the catcher twitched
a forefinger; the batter
rotated his bat
in a slow circle. But now
they pause: wary,
exact, suspended—

     while
abiding moonrise
lightens the angel
of the overgrown
garden, and Walter Blake
Adams, who died at
fourteen, waits
under the footbridge.

Donald Hall,
"The Baseball Players"

Zloto came to Havana, showed Fidel his hands, talked about the '50s. Fidel said, "They took our good men and put them in Yankee uniforms, in Bosox, Chisox, Dodgers, Birds. They took our manhood, Zloto. They took our Achilles and called him 'Archie.' Hector Gonzalez they called 'Ramrod,' Jess Ortiz they made a 'Jayo.' They treated Cuban manhood like a bowl of chicos and ricos. Yes, we have no bananas but we got vine-ripened Latinos who play good ball all year, stick their heads over the plate and wait for the Revolution. Fidel Castro gave it to them."

Max Apple, *from*
"Understanding Alvarado"

"We going to be playing a lot of white outfits too. Some of you ain't played much against white so you got to be prepared. They take what they can out of you if you don't be on your guard. They going to slide into your leg and step on your foot if you leave it out there in plain sight. They going to be saying the same old things to rattle you and get you to forget how to play right. But they ain't nothing. They got to pitch to you when you up to the plate. I hit everything a white pitch can throw and they don't like it but they can't do much but run after it. So that's how

Janet Braun-Reinitz
Report from the Fire
Zone, Scroll XV, 1986
Acrylic on paper

we play them. You keep your heads turned behind your back all the time for something sneaking up on you. That's the way you play white."

Bingo stopped again and waited for a reaction. He could feel himself getting excited.

They players sat and looked at him, blinking their eyes. Louis Keystone yawned.

"That was nice speech, Bingo. Real nice," Leon finally said.

"Yeah, thanks, Leon," Bingo said, and he sat down and pulled out a Lucky.

William Brashler, *from*
The Bingo Long Traveling All-Stars
and Motor Kings

It gets late early here

Yogi Berra

"If only there were a way of knowing . . ."
but what do you want to know? The anxiety you've
   begun
you would miss; and the consolations of chaos
can't help but continue, aware of themselves or not,
like facts you once blasted for being
pointless, which they are, only now that is a pleasure,
that there should be something beyond doubt
and certainty, pointless as a baseball score
forgotten days later, but which is now, and in the
   meanwhile,
the only important thing, win or lose, bet or no bet,
freezing at Shea because they're playing the Series
at night these days, and the man next to you, in scarf
and hood, could be your own self complaining
that nothing's the same as it was.

David Lehman,
"October Classic"

Edward Larson
Ronald Reagan Strikes Out
   on Foreign Policy, 1986
Painted wood

Feeling both mellow and unhappy—a state more common to him than he ever would have believed—Eddie skirted the building, Gucci loafers crunching in the gravel, to look at the lot where the baseball games had been played when he was a kid—when, it seemed, ninety percent of the world had been made up of kids.

The lot wasn't much changed, but a look was enough to convince him beyond doubt that the games had stopped—a tradition that had simply died out at some point in the years between, for reasons of its own.

In 1958 the diamond shape of the infield had been defined not by limed basepaths but in ruts made by running feet. They had no actual bases, those boys who had played baseball here (boys who were all older than the Losers, although Eddie remembered now that Stan Uris had sometimes played; his batting was only fair, but in the outfield he could run fast and he had the reflexes of an angel), but four pieces of dirty canvas were always kept under the loadingbay behind the long brick building, to be ceremonially taken out when enough kids had drifted into the back lot to play ball, and just as ceremonially returned when the shades of evening had fallen thickly enough to end further play.

Standing here now, Eddie could see no trace of those rutted basepaths. Weeds had grown up through the gravel in patch profusion. Broken soda and beer bottles twinkled here and there; in the old days, such shards of broken glass had been religiously removed. The only thing that was the same was the chainlink fence at the back of the lot, twelve feet high and as rusty as dried blood. It framed the sky in droves of diamond shapes.

That was home-run territory, Eddie thought, standing bemused with his hands in his pockets at the place where home plate had been twenty-seven years ago. *Over the fence and down into the Barrens. They used to call it The Automatic*. He laughed out loud and then looked around nervously, as if it were a ghost who had laughed out loud instead of a guy in sixty-dollar slacks, a guy as solid as . . . well, as solid as . . . as . . .

Get off it, Eds, Richie's voice seemed to whisper. *You ain't solid at all, and in the last few years the chucks have been few and far between. Right?*

"Yeah, right," Eddie said in a low voice, and kicked a few loose stones away in a rattle.

In truth, he had only seen two balls go over the fence at the back of the lot behind Tracker Brothers, both of them hit by the same kid: Belch Huggins. Belch had been almost comically big, already six feet tall at twelve, weighing maybe a hundred and seventy. He had gotten his nickname because he was able to articulate belches of amazing length and loudness—at his best, he sounded like a cross between a bullfrog and a cicada. Sometimes he would pat a hand rapidly across his open mouth while belching, emitting a sound like a hoarse Indian.

Belch had been big and not really fat, Eddie remembered now, but it was as if God had never really intended for a boy of twelve to attain such remarkable size; if he had not died that summer, he might have grown to six-six or better, and might have learned along the way how to maneuver his outsized body through a world of smaller denizens. He might even, Eddie thought, have learned gentleness. But at twelve he had been both clumsy and mean, not retarded but almost seeming so because all his body's actions seemed so amazingly graceless and lunging. He had none of Stanley's built-in rhythms; it was as if Belch's body did not talk to his brain at all but existed in its own cosmos of slow thunder. Eddie could remember the evening a long, slow fly ball had been hit directly to Belch's position in the outfield—Belch didn't even have to move. He stood looking up, raised his glove in an almost aimless punching gesture, and instead of settling into his glove, the ball had struck him squarely on top of the head, producing a hollow *bonk!* sound. It was as if the ball had been dropped from three stories up onto the roof of a Ford sedan. It bounced a good four feet and came down neatly into Belch's glove. An unfortunate kid named Owen Phillips had laughed at the bonking sound. Belch had walked over to him and had kicked his ass so hard that the Phillips kid had run screaming for home with a hole in the seat of his pants. No one else laughed . . . at least not on the outside. Eddie supposed that if Richie Tozier had been there, he wouldn't have been able to help it, and Belch probably would have put him in the hospital. Belch was similarly slow at the plate. He was easy to strike out, and if he hit a grounder even the most fumble-fingered infielders had no trouble throwing him out at first. But when he got all of one, it went a long, long way. The two balls Eddie had seen Belch hit over the fence had both been wonders. The first had never been recovered, although more than a dozen boys had tramped back and forth over the steeply slanting slope which plunged down into the Barrens, looking for it.

The second, however, *had* been recovered. The ball belonged to another sixthgrader (Eddie could not now remember what his real name had been, only that all the other kids called him Snuffy because he always had a cold) and had been in use for most of the late spring and early summer of '58. As a result, it was no longer the nearly perfect spherical creation of white horsehide and red stitching that it had been when it came out of the box; it was scuffed, grass-stained, and cut in several places by its hundreds of bouncing trips over the gravel in the outfield. Its stitching was beginning to come unravelled in one place, and Eddie, who shagged foul balls when his asthma wasn't too bad (relishing every casual *Thanks, kid!* when he threw the ball back to the playing field), knew that soon someone would produce a roll of Black Cat friction tape and embalm it so they could get another week or so out of it.

But before that day came, a seventhgrader with the unlikely name of Stringer Dedham tossed what he fancied a "change of speed" pitch to Belch Huggins. Belch timed the pitch perfectly (the slow ones were, you should pardon the pun, just his speed) and hit Snuffy's elderly Spalding so hard that the cover came right off and fluttered down just a few feet shy of second base like a big white moth. The ball itself had continued up and up into a gorgeous twilit sky, unravelling and unravelling as it went, kids turning to follow its progress in dumb wonder; up and over the chainlink fence it went, still rising, and Eddie remembered Stringer Dedham had said, "Ho-ly shit!" in a soft and awestruck voice as it went, riding a track into the sky, and they had all seen the unwinding string, and maybe even before it hit, six boys had been monkeying up that fence, and Eddie could remember Tony Tracker laughing in an amazed loonlike way and crying: "That one would have been out of Yankee Stadium! Do you hear me? That one would have been out of *fucking Yankee Stadium!*"

It had been Peter Gordon who found the ball, not far from the stream the Losers' Club would dam up less than three weeks later. What was left was not even three inches through the center; it was some kind of cockeyed miracle that the twine had never broken.

By unspoken consent, the boys had brought the remains of Snuffy's ball back to Tony Tracker, who examined it without saying a word, surrounded by boys who were likewise silent. Seen from a distance that circle of boys standing around the tall man with the big sloping belly might have seemed almost religious in its intent—the veneration of a holy object. Belch Huggins had not even run around the bases. He only stood among the others like a boy who had no precise idea of where he was. What Tony Tracker handed him that day was smaller than a tennis ball.

Eddie, lost in these memories, walked from the place where home had been, across the pitcher's mound (only it had never been a mound; it had been a depression from which the gravel had been scraped clean), and out into shortstop country. He paused briefly, struck by the silence, and then strolled on out to the chainlink fence. It was rustier than ever, and overgrown by some sort of ugly climbing vine, but still there. Looking through it, he could see how the ground sloped away, aggressively green.

Stephen King, from
It

Baseball's time is seamless and invisible, a bubble within which players move at exactly the same pace and rhythms as all their predecessors. This is the way the game was played in our youth and in our father's youth, and even back then— back in the country days— there must have been the same feeling that time could be stopped. Since baseball time is measured only in outs, all you have to do is succeed utterly; keep hitting, keep the rally alive, and you have defeated time. You remain forever young.

Roger Angell, *from*
The Summer Game

Joel Meyerowitz
Provincetown, 1977
Photograph

I remember the Chillicothe ball players grappling the Rock Island ball
  players in a sixteen-inning game ended by darkness.
And the shoulders of the Chillicothe players were a red smoke against the
  sundown and the shoulders of the Rock Island players were a yellow
  smoke against the sundown.
And the umpire's voice was hoarse calling balls and strikes and outs and
  the umpire's throat fought in the dust for a song.

Carl Sandburg,
"Hits and Runs"

Long ago I passed the point in life when major-league ballplayers begin to be younger than yourself. Now all of them are, except for a few aging trigenarians and a couple of quadros who don't get around on the fastball as well as they used to and who sit out the second games of doubleheaders. However, despite my age (thirty-nine), I am still active and have a lot of interests. One of them is slow-pitch softball, a game that lets me go through the motions of baseball without getting beaned or having to run too hard. I play on a pretty casual team, one that drinks beer on the bench and substitutes freely. If a player's wife or girlfriend wants to play, we give her a glove and send her out to right field, no questions asked,

and if she lets a pop fly drop six feet in front of her, nobody agonizes over it.

Except me. This year. For the first time in my life, just as I am entering the dark twilight of my slow-pitch career, I find myself taking the game seriously. It isn't the bonehead play that bothers me especially—the pop fly that drops untouched, the slow roller juggled and the ball then heaved ten feet over the first baseman's head and into the next diamond, the routine singles that go through outfielders' legs for doubles and triples with gloves flung after them. No, it isn't our stone-glove fielding or pussyfoot base-running or limp-wristed hitting that gives me fits, though these have put us on the short end of some mighty

ridiculous scores this summer. It's our attitude.

Bottom of the ninth, down 18-3, two outs, a man on first and a woman on third, and our third baseman strikes out. *Strikes out!* In slow-pitch, not even your grandmother strikes out, but this guy does, and after his third strike—a wild swing at a ball that bounces on the plate—he topples over in the dirt and lies flat on his back, laughing. *Laughing!*

Same game, earlier. They have the bases loaded. A weak grounder is hit toward our second baseperson. The runners are running. She picks up the ball, and she looks at them. She looks at first, at second, at home. We yell, "Throw it! Throw it!" and she throws it, underhand, at the pitcher, who has turned and run to back up the catcher. The ball rolls across the thirdbase line and under the bench. Three runs score. The batter, a fatso, chugs into second. The other team hoots and hollers, and what does she do? She shrugs and smiles ("Oh, silly me"); after all, it's only a game. Like the aforementioned strikeout artist, she treats her error as a joke. They have forgiven themselves instantly, which is unforgivable. It is *we* who should forgive them, who can say, "It's all right, it's only a game." They are supposed to throw up their hands and kick the dirt and hang their heads, as if this boner, even if it is their sixteenth of the afternoon —*this* is the one that really and truly breaks their hearts.

That attitude sweetens the game for everyone. The sinner feels sweet remorse. The fatso feels some sense of accomplishment; this is no bunch of rumdums he forced into an error but a team with some class. We, the sinner's teammates, feel momentary anger at her— dumb! dumb play!—but then, seeing her grief, we sympathize with her in our hearts (any one of us might have made that mistake or one worse), and we yell encouragement, including the shortstop, who, moments

before, dropped an easy throw for a force at second. "That's all right! Come on! We got 'em!" we yell. "Shake it off! These turkeys can't hit!" This makes us all feel good, even though the turkeys now lead us by ten runs. We're getting clobbered, but we have a winning attitude.

Let me say this about attitude: Each player is responsible for his or her own attitude, and to a considerable degree you can *create* a good attitude by doing certain little things on the field. These are certain little things that ballplayers do in the Bigs, and we ought to be doing them in the Slows.

1. When going up to bat, don't step right into the batter's box as if it were an elevator. The box is your turf, your stage. Take possession of it slowly and deliberately, starting with a lot of back-bending, knee-stretching, and torso-revolving in the on-deck circle. Then, approaching the box, stop outside it and tap the dirt off your spikes with your bat. You don't have spikes, you have sneakers, of course, but the significance of the tapping is the same. Then, upon entering the box, spit on the ground. It's a way of saying, "This here is mine. This is where I get my hits."

2. Spit frequently. Spit at all crucial moments. Spit correctly. Spit should be *blown*, not ptuied weakly with the lips, which often results in dribble. Spitting should convey forcefulness of purpose, concentration, pride. Spit down, not in the direction of others. Spit in the glove and on the fingers, especially after making a real knucklehead play; it's a way of saying, "I dropped the ball because my glove was dry."

3. At bat and in the field, pick up dirt. Rub dirt in the fingers (especially after spitting on them). Toss dirt, as if testing the wind for velocity and direction. Smooth the dirt. Be involved with dirt. If·no dirt is available (e.g., in the outfield), pluck tufts of grass. Fielders should be grooming their areas constantly between plays, flicking away tiny sticks and bits of gravel.

4. Take your time. Tie your laces. Confer with your teammates about possible situations that may arise and conceivable options in dealing with them. Extend the game. Three errors on three consecutive plays can be humiliating if the plays occur within the space of a couple of minutes, but if each error is separated from the next by extensive conferences on the mound, lace-tying, glove ad-

Neal Slavin

Women's Intramural Softball Team of Warner Communications, Inc., NY, NY, 1979
Color coupler print

justments, and arguing close calls (if any), the effect on morale is minimized.

5. Talk. Not just an occasional "Let's get a hit now" but continuous rhythmic chatter, a flow of syllables: "Hey babe hey babe c'mon babe good stick now hey babe long tater take him downtown babe . . . hey good eye good eye."

Infield chatter is harder to maintain. Since the slow-pitch pitch is required to be a soft underhand lob, infielders hesitate to say, "Smoke him babe hey low heat hey throw it on the black babe chuck it in there back him up babe no hit no hit." Say it anyway.

6. One final rule, perhaps the most important of all: When your team is up and has made the third out, the batter and the players who were left on base do not come back to the bench for their gloves. *They remain on the field, and their teammates bring their gloves out to them.* This requires some organization and discipline, but it pays off big in morale. It says, "Although we're getting our pants knocked off, still we must conserve our energy."

Imagine that you have bobbled two fly balls in this rout and now you have just tried to stretch a single into a double and have been easily thrown out sliding into second base, where the base runner ahead of you had stopped. It was the third out and a dumb play, and your opponents smirk at you as they run off the field. You are the goat, a lonely and tragic figure sitting in the dirt. You curse yourself, jerking your head sharply forward. You stand up and kick the base. How miserable! How degrading! Your utter shame, though brief, bears silent testimony to the worthiness of your teammates, whom you have let down, and they appreciate it. They call out to you now as they take the field, and as the second baseman runs to his position he says, "Let's get 'em now," and tosses you your glove. Lowering your head, you trot slowly out to right. There you do some deep knee bends. You pick grass. You find a pebble and fling it into foul territory. As the first batter comes to the plate, you check the sun. You get set in your stance, poised to fly. Feet spread, hands on hips, you bend slightly at the waist and spit the expert spit of a veteran ballplayer—a player who has known the agony of defeat but who always bounces back, a player who has lost a stride on the base paths but can still make the big play.

This is *ball*, ladies and gentlemen. This is what it's all about.

Garrison Keillor,
"Attitude"

Checklist of the Exhibition

This checklist represents the exhibition as it appeared at the New York State Museum in Albany, New York from September 16 to November 15, 1987. Several substitutions are being made for the national tour. *Sizes are indicated in inches, height by width by depth.*

Nicholas Africano
Ernie Banks, 1979
Oil, acrylic, wax, and
    canvas on masonite
13 x 32½
Collection of Mr. and Mrs.
    Douglas Cohen

Mauro Altamura
Untitled, 1984
Photograph
30 x 40
Collection of the artist

Anonymous
Untitled
Oil on canvas
16 x 23½
The Gladstone Collection
    of Baseball Art

Anonymous
Weathervane, no date
Copper
21 x 33 x 4
Private collection

Anonymous
*Brooklyn Baltics vs.
    Liberty Nine of New
    Brunswick*, 1870-72
Watercolor on cloth
23 x 30
Collection of T. Dennie
    Williams and his
    father, Thomas D.
    Williams

Richard Artschwager
Untitled (Set of 6 baseball
    drawings), 1969
Graphite on paper
25 x 19 (each drawing)
Courtesy of Paula Cooper
    Gallery, New York

George Wesley Bellows
The Baseball Game,
    c. 1908
Oil on canvas
16 x 20½
Collection of Muskegon
    Museum of Art

Gerry Bergstein
My Turn at Bat, 1987
Oil on canvas
96 x 8
Collection of the artist;
    courtesy of Stux
    Gallery

Janet Braun-Reinitz
*Report from the Fire
    Zone, Scroll XV*, 1986
Acrylic on paper
96 x 48
Collection of the artist

Harvey Breverman
Beckett and Baseball,
    1986
Pastel on paper
22 x 31
Collection of the artist

Marilyn Bridges
*Playing Baseball, Allens
    Creek, NY*, 1986
Photograph
16 x 20
Collection of the artist

David Burnett
From *Pre-game in the
    Sally League*, 1981
Photograph
13½ x 9
Courtesy of Contact Press
    Images, New York

Tina Chaden
The Baseball Fan, 1985
Paper, clay, and egg
    tempera
15 x 40 x 30
Collection of the artist

James Chapin
*Veteran Bush League
    Catcher*, 1948
Oil on canvas
50 x 40
Collection of Dale C.
    Bullough

Ron Cohen
Willie Mays, 1978
Acrylic and oil on canvas
68 x 64
Collection of Barry C.
    Scheck and Lawrence
    A. Vogelman

James Daugherty
Three Base Hit, 1914
Gouache and ink on paper
12¼ x 17¼
Collection of The Whitney
    Museum of American
    Art, New York.
    Purchase

Elbert Davis
Death of an Umpire, no
    date
Oil on linen
21½ x 41
Collection of Italo Scanga
    and Stephanie
    Smedley Scanga

Rupert Deese
Whiteness of the Whale,
    1984
Oil on canvas
50 x 38
Collection of Linda
    Komaroff

Elaine de Kooning
Campy at the Plate,
    1953-80
Acrylic on canvas
30 x 39
Collection of the artist

Claudia DeMonte
*Claudia at Doubleday
    Field*, 1984
Pulp, paper, acrylic, and
    mixed media
12 x 14
Courtesy of Gracie
    Mansion Gallery

Jed Devine
Untitled (Cups and
    baseball book), 1985
Palladium print
10 x 8
Courtesy of Bonni
    Benrubi Fine Art
    Photographs

Jed Devine
Untitled (Kitchen wall
    with Babe Ruth
    postcard), 1985
Palladium print
10 x 8
Courtesy of Bonni
    Benrubi Fine Art
    Photographs

Harvey Dinnerstein
The Wide Swing, 1974
Oil on canvas
24 x 32
Collection of Phil Desind,
    on loan to The Butler
    Institute of American
    Art, Youngstown, Ohio

John Dobbs
Follow Thru,
    c. 1978
Watercolor on paper
4 x 4
Courtesy of ACA
    Galleries, New York

John Dobbs
Stretching at First,
    c. 1976
Oil on canvas
36 x 40
Courtesy of ACA
    Galleries, New York

Steve Donegan
The Champions, 1985
Glazed earthenware
12 x 10 x 10
Collection of the artist

Jim Dow
*Charlotte Hornets
    Ballpark*, 1981
Color coupler prints (4)
8 x 38
Collection of the artist

Jim Dow
*County Stadium,
    Milwaukee*, 1982
Color coupler prints (3)
8 x 28½
Collection of the artist

Jim Dow
Durham Bulls Ballpark,
    1981
Color coupler prints (3)
9½ x 23½
Collection of the artist

Jim Dow
Houston Astrodome, 1982
Color coupler prints (3)
9½ x 23½
Collection of the artist

John Dreyfuss
Catcher, 1984
Bronze (edition of 12)
14 x 12 x 16
Courtesy of Fendrick
    Gallery, Washington,
    DC

John Dreyfuss
Pitcher, 1984
Bronze (edition of 12)
33 x 16 x 16
Courtesy of Fendrick
    Gallery, Washington,
    DC

Leonard Dufresne
Injured Catcher, 1975
Acrylic on masonite
6 x 5
Collection of Sydney and
    Frances Lewis

Leonard Dufresne
Man on Second, 1975
Acrylic on masonite
9 x 6
Collection of Sydney and
    Frances Lewis

Raoul Dufy
Ball Park—Boston,
    c. 1950
Watercolor
19½ x 25½
Collection of Rose Art
    Museum, Brandeis
    University, Waltham,
    Massachusetts; gift of
    Mr. and Mrs. Edwin E.
    Hokin, Highland Park,
    Illinois

Philip Evergood
*The Early Youth of Babe
    Ruth*, c. 1939
Oil on canvas
20 x 24
Collection of Hirshhorn
    Museum and
    Sculpture Garden,
    Smithsonian
    Institution; gift of
    Joseph H. Hirshhorn

Ralph Fasanella
*Night Game—Yankee
    Stadium*, 1961
Oil on canvas
60 x 74
Collection of the artist

Ralph Fasanella
Sandlot Game, 1954
Oil on canvas
36 x 40
Collection of Mr. and Mrs.
    John DePolo

Eric Fischl
Boys at Bat, 1979
Oil on canvas
84 x 69
Collection of Edwin L.
    Stringer, Q.C.

Vernon Fisher
Baseball Cap, 1977
Photograph with rhoplex
22 x 39½
Collection of Diann and
    Ned Rifkin

Arnold Friedman
World Series, c. 1930-38
Oil on canvas
20 x 23
The Phillips Collection,
    Washington, DC

Charles Garabedian
Baseball, 1965
Flo-paque on paper
36 x 77
Private collection

Gerald Garston
Pastime, 1984
Oil on canvas
60 x 46
Collection of Norman and
    Ruthellen Gahm

Gerald Garston
Spring Training, 1981
Oil on canvas
40 x 49
Collection of The Law
    Firm of Wiggin &
    Dana, New Haven,
    Connecticut

Cristos Gianakos
*Six Altered Baseball
    Stadium Post Cards*,
    1985
Collage
3½ x 5½ (each collage)
Collection of the artist

Steve Gianakos
Untitled, 1981
Acrylic on canvas
34 x 24
Courtesy of Barbara Toll
    Fine Arts, New York

Sidney Goodman
Tryout, 1965
Oil on canvas
35 x 24½
Collection of Mrs. Janet
    H. Shands

Susan Grayson
*Rickey Henley
    Henderson*, 1985
Photographs (16 images)
17 x 36½ (matted)
Collection of the artist;
    published by Baseball
    Action Shots Annual

Susan Grayson
Gaylord Jackson Perry,
    1983
Photographs (35 images)
27½ x 36½ (matted)
Collection of the artist;
    published by Baseball
    Action Shots Annual

Susan Grayson
Joseph Chris Carter, 1986
Photographs (13 images)
17 x 36½ (matted)
Collection of the artist;
    published by Baseball
    Action Shots Annual

Red Grooms
Expos in the Rain, 1985
Gouache on paper (5
    sheets)
17 x 70
Collection of Lysiane
    Luong and Red
    Grooms

Robert Gwathmey
World Series, 1958
Oil on canvas
32 x 45
Courtesy of Terry
    Dintenfass, Inc.

Robert Gwathmey
World Series #2, 1958
Watercolor and pencil on
    paper
29 x 21
Courtesy of Terry
    Dintenfass, Inc.

Lewis Hine
*Playground in a
    Tenement Alley,
    Boston*, 1909
Photograph (modern
    print from original
    negative)
6½ x 9½
Collection of
    International Museum
    of Photography at
    George Eastman
    House

Michael Hurson
Baseball Player (at bat),
    1982
Pencil, pastel, ink, and
    conte crayon on paper
21 x 16½
Collection of Elizabeth
    Murray, New York

Walter Iooss, Jr.
*Little League, East
    Orange, NJ*, 1965
Photograph
14 x 11
Courtesy of Walter Iooss,
    Jr./Sports Illustrated

Walter Iooss, Jr.
*Three-Quarter Century
    League Softball, St.
    Petersburg, Florida*,
    1973
Photograph
14 x 11
Courtesy of Walter Iooss,
    Jr./Sports Illustrated

Jane Irish
*Shea Stadium is the New
    York Mets and the
    New York Mets are
    Shea Stadium*, 1984
Egg tempera on board/
    cardboard
44 x 52 x 12
Courtesy of Sharpe
    Gallery

Andy Jurinko
Wrigley Field, 1983
Charcoal and pastel on
    paper
30 x 44
Courtesy of Gallery
    Henoch

Jacob Kass
Picking a Team, 1985
Oil on saw blade
7 x 27½
Collection of Penny
    McCall

Alex Katz
Baseball Figure, 1980
Aluminum, electric
    motor, and scrim
23 x 13½ x ¹⁄₁₆ (before
    installation)
Collection of the artist

Lavern Kelley
*Bass Wood of the
    Tinkerville Tomcats*,
    1987
Enamel paint and wood
18 x 7 x 7
Collection of the artist

John Kennard
New York, NY, 1983
Photograph
14½ x 18
Collection of the artist

John Kennard
Shea Stadium, New York,
    1983
Photograph
23½ x 30
Collection of the artist

Basil King
Pastorale, 1983
Oil on canvas
35 x 49
Collection of the artist

William King
Self as Doubleday, 1986
Red vinyl
81 x 31 x 30
Courtesy of Terry
    Dintenfass, Inc.

Robert Kushner
LA Dodgers, 1978
Watercolor on paper
67 x 30
Collecton of Thomas B.
    Solomon

Leslie Kuter
*Autobiographical Art
    History: Eakins
    Concert Singer,
    Queen Hatshepsut,
    and Josh Gibson*, 1978
Wool on burlap
69 x 51
Collection of the artist

Michael Langenstein
Astro-Turf, 1983
Postcard collage
4 x 6
Collection of the artist

Michael Langenstein
Play Ball, 1982
Postcard collage
4 x 6
Collection of Mr. and Mrs.
    Samuel A. Ramirez

Michael Langenstein
Yangtze Stadium, 1983
Postcard collage
3½ x 6
Collection of the artist

Edward Larson
*Ronald Reagan Strikes
    Out on Foreign Policy*,
    1986
Painted wood
26 x 35½ x 16
Courtesy of Zolla/
    Lieberman Gallery

Jacob Lawrence
Strike, 1949
Tempera on masonite
20 x 24
Collection of Howard
    University Gallery of
    Art

Helen Levitt
New York, 1972
Dye transfer photograph
11 x 14
Courtesy of Laurence
    Miller Gallery

Kim MacConnell
Green Sliding, 1980
Two-color silkscreen on
    diecut and folded
    paper (from a set of 3)
14½ x 22
Courtesy of Holly
    Solomon Gallery

Deryl Daniel Mackie
Smokey Joe Williams,
    1985
Acrylic on canvas
64 x 54
Collection of the artist

John Marin
Baseball, 1953
Colored pencil on paper
8½ x 10½
The Gladstone Collection
    of Baseball Art

**Jim Markowich and Paul
    Kuhrman**
*The Ace of Bases (from
    the Tarot de
    Cooperstown)*, 1983
Acrylic and colored pencil
    on canvas
26 x 14
Collection of Jim
    Markowich

**Jim Markowich and Paul
    Kuhrman**
*The Ace of Bats (from the
    Tarot de
    Cooperstown)*, 1983
Acrylic and colored pencil
    on canvas
26 x 14
Collection of Jim
    Markowich

**Jim Markowich and Paul
    Kuhrman**
*The Round Tripper (from
    the Tarot de
    Cooperstown)*, 1983
Acrylic and colored pencil
    on canvas
26 x 14
Collection of Jim
    Markowich

Jim Markowich
*The Nondenominational
    Church of St. Babe*,
    1985-87
Wood, brass, plastic, and
    film
29 x 24 x 36
Collection of the artist

Justin McCarthy
Yankees Win Series, 4-3
    (5 separate paintings),
    1952
Watercolor on board
24½ x 30½ (with mat)
The Gladstone Collection
    of Baseball Art

Richard Merkin
*Self-Portrait as a Relief
    Pitcher for the
    Rochester Red-Wings*,
    1985
Pastel on paper
12 x 9
The Gladstone Collection
    of Baseball Art

Joel Meyerowitz
Provincetown, 1977
Photograph
15½ x 19½
Collection of Sasha
    Meyerowitz

Joel Meyerowitz
*Busch Stadium and the
    Arch*, 1978
Photograph
15½ x 19½
Collection of Ariel
    Meyerowitz

Scott Mlyn
*Before the Game, Dodger
    Stadium, Los Angeles*,
    1985
Photograph
8 x 12
Collection of the artist

Scott Mlyn
*Ron Cey, Wrigley Field,
    Chicago*, 1986
Photograph
12 x 8
Collection of the artist

Scott Mlyn
*Two Fans and Wally
    Joyner, Memorial
    Stadium, Baltimore*,
    1986
Photograph
12 x 8
Collection of the artist

Scott Mlyn
*Yankee and Fans, Yankee
    Stadium, New York*,
    1980
Photograph
8 x 12
Collection of the artist

Nickolas Muray
Babe Ruth, c. 1938
Photograph (modern
    print from original
    negative)
9½ x 7½
Collection of
    International Museum
    of Photography at
    George Eastman
    House

Nicholas Nixon
*Adams Street,
    Watertown, MA*, 1977
Photograph
8 x 10
Collection of the artist

Jim Nutt
Ron Kittle, 1985
Colored pencil on paper
20 x 16
Collection of Mr. and Mrs.
    John LeBourgeois

Claes Oldenburg
*Bat Spinning at the
    Speed of Light*, 1975
Lithograph
34 x 21
Courtesy of Landfall Press
    Inc.

Claes Oldenburg
Mitt, 1973
Lithograph
13 x 15
Courtesy of Landfall Press
    Inc.

Joel Otterson
Fetish Perfect, 1985
Wood, iron, steel, and
    copper
100 x 11 x 11
Collection of John Sacchi,
    New York; courtesy of
    Gallery Nature Morte,
    New York

Tod Papageorge
Shea Stadium, 1970
Gelatin-silver print
8⅛ x 12¹⁄₁₆
Collection of The
    Museum of Modern
    Art, New York; gift of
    the photographer.
    John Parkinson III
    Fund

Ed Paschke
Mask Man, 1970
Lithograph
12 x 6
Collection of the artist;
    courtesy of Phyllis
    Kind Gallery

Howardena Pindell
*Baseball Series: Video
    Drawing*, 1974-76
Color photograph
11 x 14
Collection of the artist

Howardena Pindell
*Baseball Series: Video
    Drawing*, 1974-76
Color photograph
11 x 14
Collection of the artist

Andrew Radcliffe
The Baseball Game, 1986
Oil on canvas
18 x 22
Courtesy of Nancy
    Hoffman Gallery, New
    York

Robert Rauschenberg
Rank, 1964
Lithograph
16 x 16
Collection of the artist

Lance Richbourg
*Untitled (Upended
    Catcher)*, 1978
Oil on canvas
83 x 99
Private collection, Kings
    Point, New York

Nelson Rosenberg
Out at Third, no date
Watercolor and gouache
15 x 22
The Phillips Collection,
    Washington, DC

Mark Rucker
*Angel Hermosa's Double
    Play*, 1974
Graphite on paper
27½ x 22
Collection of The
    University at Albany,
    State University of
    New York

Italo Scanga
Meta VII: Thoughts on Baseball, 1986
Oil paint and lacquer on wood, musical instruments
81½ x 27 x 25
Collection of Italo Scanga and Stephanie Smedley Scanga

Vincent Scilla
Spring Training in the Mountains, 1985
Oil on canvas
20 x 24
Collection of the artist

Stephen Shore
Graig Nettles, Fort Lauderdale Yankee Stadium, Fort Lauderdale, Florida, 1978
Photograph
8 x 10
Collection of the artist; courtesy of Pace/MacGill Gallery

Clyde Singer
Minor League, 1946
Oil on canvas
40 x 50
Collection of The Butler Institute of American Art, Youngstown, Ohio

Neal Slavin
Women's Intramural Softball Team of Warner Communications, Inc., NY, NY, 1979
Color coupler print
10½ x 10½
Collection of the artist

Buzz Spector
Comiskey Park, 1985
Pastel and paper relief
8 x 10
Collection of Bruce A. Ruzgis

James Sullivan
Game Ball, 1987
Charcoal on paper
30 x 22
Courtesy of Nancy Hoffman Gallery, New York

Gregory Thorp
Triple A-143, 1979
Cibachrome photograph
13 x 19½
Courtesy of Carl Solway Gallery, Cincinnati

Sidney Tillim
A Dream of Being, 1968-69
Oil on canvas
72 x 90
Collection of the artist

Andy Warhol
Pete Rose, 1985
Screenprint
40 x 31
Courtesy of Carl Solway Gallery, Cincinnati

Margaret Wharton
Bat-e, 1985
Wood and epoxy
15 x 14 x 2
Collection of Phyllis Kind, New York

Karl Wirsum
Looking for a Curveball in Cuernavaca, 1983
Acrylic on canvas
44 x 49
Collection of Krannert Art Museum, University of Illinois, Champaign

Lenders to the Exhibition

ACA Galleries, New York
Mauro Altamura
Bonni Benrubi Fine Art Photographs, New York
Gerry Bergstein
Janet Braun-Reinitz
Harvey Breverman
Marilyn Bridges
Dale C. Bullough
The Butler Institute of American Art, Youngstown, Ohio
Susan Cahan
Tina Chaden
Mr. and Mrs. Douglas Cohen
Contact Press Images, New York
Paula Cooper Gallery, New York
Elaine de Kooning
Mr. and Mrs. John DePolo
Phil Desind
Terry Dintenfass, Inc., New York
Steve Donegan
Jim Dow
Ralph Fasanella
Fendrick Gallery, Washington, DC
Norman and Ruthellen Gahm
Cristos Gianakos
The Gladstone Collection of Baseball Art

Susan Grayson
Gallery Henoch
Hirshhorn Museum and Sculpture Garden, Smithsonian Institution, Washington, DC
Nancy Hoffman Gallery, New York
Howard University Gallery of Art, Washington, DC
International Museum of Photography at George Eastman House, Rochester
Walter Iooss, Jr.
Alex Katz
Lavern Kelley
John Kennard
Phyllis Kind
Basil King
Linda Komaroff
Krannert Art Museum, University of Illinois, Champaign
Leslie Kuter
Landfall Press Inc., Chicago
Michael Langenstein
Mr. and Mrs. John LeBourgeois
Sydney and Frances Lewis
Anne Liuet
Lysiane Luong and Red Grooms
Deryl Daniel Mackie
Gracie Mansion Gallery
Jim Markowich
Penny McCall
Ariel Meyerowitz
Sasha Meyerowitz
Laurence Miller Gallery, New York
Scott Mlyn
Elizabeth Murray
The Museum of Modern Art, New York
Muskegon Museum of Art, Muskegon, Michigan
Nicholas Nixon
The Phillips Collection, Washington, DC
Howardena Pindell
Mr. and Mrs. Samuel A. Ramirez
Robert Rauschenberg
Diann and Ned Rifkin
Rose Art Museum, Brandeis University, Waltham, Massachusetts
Bruce A. Ruzgis
Italo Scanga and Stephanie Smedley Scanga
Barry C. Scheck and Lawrence A. Vogelman
Vincent Scilla
Janet H. Shands
Sharpe Gallery, New York
Stephen Shore
Neal Slavin
Holly Solomon Gallery, New York

Thomas B. Solomon
Carl Solway Gallery, Cincinnati
Buzz Spector
Sports Illustrated
Edwin L. Stringer, Q.C.
Sidney Tillim
Barbara Toll Fine Arts, New York
The University at Albany, State University of New York
The Whitney Museum of American Art, New York
Wiggin & Dana, New Haven, Connecticut
T. Dennie Williams and Thomas D. Williams
Karl Wirsum
Zolla/Lieberman Gallery, Chicago
and numerous private collectors.

Photography Credits

The numbers in parentheses refer to page numbers.

Gregory Benson (136)
Geoffrey Clements (117)
D. James Dee (106)
Marty Fumo (54, 55, 75)
Herb Gallagher (19)
Charles Kelley, Jr. (back cover, 66)
Dennis McWaters (105, 123)
Tom Moore (143)
Edward Owen (84)
R. Porello (41l, 151)
Adam Reich (58-59, 83, 124)
Dan Soper (41r)
Lee Stalsworth (52)
David Wynne (9, 38)
Zindman/Fremont (146-147,150)

164

Curatorial Acknowledgments

An exhibition and publication of this scope could not have succeeded without the dedication of a great many individuals. As they say in baseball, it was indeed a "team effort." There are too many on this team to list individually, but several must be singled out for their special efforts.

To our partners at SITES (Smithsonian Institution Traveling Exhibition Service), we extend our sincere appreciation for their invaluable assistance throughout the project. It was a pleasure working with Eileen Rose, Andrea Stevens, and the entire staff. Also our appreciation to Diana Duke Duncan, Maria Downs, and Bowie Kuhn for their early support and efforts on the project.

A special thank you must go to certain colleagues who generously shared their expertise with us. Whenever we needed advice, these people were always there: Nina Felshin, John Gilmartin of NBC Sports, Bill Goff, Nancy Green, Ivan Karp, Jim LaVilla-Havelin, David Resnicow and Fred Schroeder of Arts & Communications Counselors, Patterson Sims, John Stadler, and Robin White.

Our appreciation also goes to the following people who contributed in a variety of ways to the successful completion of this exhibition and book: Richard Armstrong, Amy Barnum, Roberta Bernstein, Douglas Blau, Janet Borden, Bruce Chambers, Peter Clark, Marijo Dougherty, Sheryl Epstein, Fred Escher, Susan Grayson, John Hanhardt, Peter Irving, Caroline Keck, Bruce Kurtz, Thomas Lavrinos, Gracie Mansion, Tim Metallo, Dewey Mosby, Gwendolyn Owens, Robert Perlow, Anne Resnick, Patty Kerr Ross, Mark Rucker, David Shapiro, Joel Shapiro, Lin Smith, Tom Solomon, John Thorn, Gib Vincent, Gladys Ann Wells, and William Zimmer.

Other individuals, associated with institutions, who were valuable resources include: Miles Barth at the International Center of Photography, Susan Brundage at Leo Castelli Gallery, Carol Celentano at Phyllis Kind Gallery in New York, Paula Cooper of the Paula Cooper Gallery, John Froats at Daniel Wolf Gallery, Suzanne Ghez and Pat Scott at The Renaissance Society in Chicago, Nancy Hoffman of the Nancy Hoffman Gallery, Karen Loveland at the Museum of American History, and Beth Moore at Terry Dintenfass, Inc.

In doing our research for the literary selections, the following books were of special assistance to us: *The Fireside Book of Baseball* series, edited by Charles Einstein; *Baseball, I Gave You All the Best Years of My Life*, edited by Kevin Kerrane and Richard Grossinger; and *The Interior Diamond: Baseball in Twentieth Century Poetry and Fiction* (Doctoral Thesis at University of Colorado) by Patrick Allen Knisley.

Our goal from the beginning was to reach as broad and diverse an audience as possible with this exhibition. The national tour is one way toward that goal. The production of this publication is another; to Nion McEvoy at Chronicle Books, we extend our gratitude for his conviction and commitment to making this publication a reality. Also thanks to the fine staff at Chronicle Books, including David Barich, Jack Jensen, and Mary Ann Gilderbloom. In Albany, special acknowledgments to Cathie Gifford for her work on the manuscript and to John Yost of our Museum staff for his expert photographic work for the book.

To Michael Donovan of Donovan and Green Marketing Communications, a special thanks for his creative work on the exhibition's graphics. And to Dare Porter of Dare Porter/Graphic Design, San Francisco, our gratitude for such fine work on the publication.

To our corporate sponsors, American Express Company, we extend our deepest appreciation for their belief in and support of the exhibition and national tour. It was a pleasure to get to know and work with Susan Bloom at American Express. Her enthusiasm and guidance throughout were vital elements to the project's final success. Thanks also to Anne Wickham at American Express.

For colleagues at the State Museum, it is probably enough thanks merely to say "we did it." (And did it well). But a special acknowledgment must go to Grace Kraus and Rosemary Malinowski for their tireless efforts on the sometimes overwhelming amount of secretarial details. Also, my special thanks to Christine Sadowski, who became my assistant late in the project, and brought a fresh energy and enthusiasm to all the various tasks she was asked to work on.

We owe a great debt to Bob Sullivan, Director of the Division of Museum Services at the New York State Museum, who, while not actually listed as a curator for the exhibition, was an ever-present figure—advising, guiding, adjudicating . . . His efforts on the project were immeasurable.

Our deep appreciation and gratitude to all the lenders (listed on a separate page) who so generously agreed to share their work with the public. And finally, a very special thank you to all the artists and writers—for creating these works and sharing their vision with us.

Peter H. Gordon, with
Sydney Waller and
Paul Weinman

Permissions